# 20TH CENTURY ROCK AND ROLL
# PROGRESSIVE ROCK

## Jerry Lucky

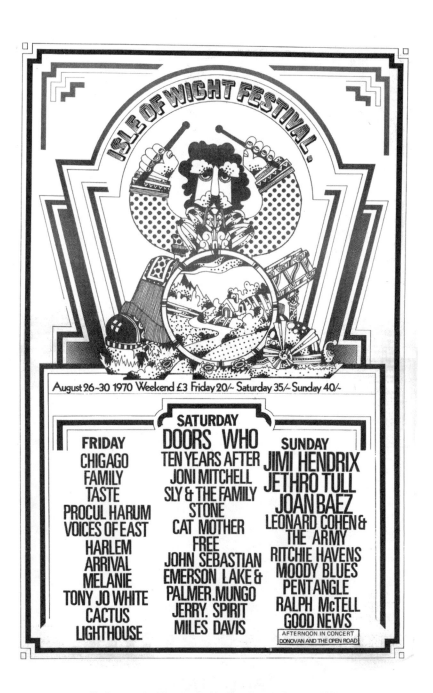

ISLE OF WIGHT FESTIVAL.

August 26~30 1970 Weekend £3 Friday 20/- Saturday 35/- Sunday 40/-

**SATURDAY**

| FRIDAY | DOORS WHO | SUNDAY |
|---|---|---|
| CHIGAGO | TEN YEARS AFTER | JIMI HENDRIX |
| FAMILY | JONI MITCHELL | JETHRO TULL |
| TASTE | SLY & THE FAMILY | JOAN BAEZ |
| PROCUL HARUM | STONE | LEONARD COHEN & |
| VOICES OF EAST | CAT MOTHER | THE ARMY |
| HARLEM | FREE | RITCHIE HAVENS |
| ARRIVAL | JOHN SEBASTIAN | MOODY BLUES |
| MELANIE | EMERSON LAKE & | PENTANGLE |
| TONY JO WHITE | PALMER.MUNGO | RALPH McTELL |
| CACTUS | JERRY. SPIRIT | GOOD NEWS |
| LIGHTHOUSE | MILES DAVIS | AFTERNOON IN CONCERT DONOVAN AND THE OPEN ROAD |

All rights reserved under article two of the Berne Copyright Convention (1971).
No part of this book may be reproduced or transmitted in any form or by any means,
electronic or mechanical, including photocopying, recording, or by any information storage
and retrieval system without permission in writing from the publisher.
We acknowledge the financial support of the Government of Canada through
the Book Publishing Industry Development Program for our publishing activities.
Published by Collector's Guide Publishing Inc., Box 62034, Burlington, Ontario, Canada, L7R 4K2
Printed and bound in Canada
20th Century Rock and Roll - Progressive Rock
by Jerry Lucky
ISBN 1-896522-20-3

# 20TH CENTURY ROCK AND ROLL

# PROGRESSIVE ROCK

## Jerry Lucky

# Table of Contents

# Dedication

To my wife Sue, my daughter Rachel, and to all the music critics who took the time to slam a genre they never understood.

# Acknowledgments

As with any book, it's rarely a one person show, and that means there are many unknowns who work behind the scenes and that need to be thanked. Researching a book such as this requires tracking down a lot of specifics as they relate to the bands selected. So, a big thank you needs to go out to all those who've created information packed web sites, magazine articles and record company puff pieces on the groups or individuals I've chosen as the most influential progressive rock bands. All of these sources came in handy. In particular I'd like to thank John Collinge at Progression and Peter Thelen at Expose. Both of these first-rate publications were wonderful sources of background material on some of the artists included here. On the record company side, Joyce at Cuneiform Records was extremely helpful, as was Dave at CMC International. Thanks needs to go out to all the photographers who recorded the visual side of the many progressive rock bands through the decades. The photographs used here are from a wide variety of sources including record company files, tour books, web sites, and, in a few cases, personal photos. In that regard, thanks to Juan Joy (Cast), Monique Froese (Tangerine Dream), Jim Rakete (Tangerine Dream) and of course dozens of record company photographers. And once again a big thanks to the Robert Godwin, Ric Connors and the gang at CG Publishing for giving me the opportunity add one more piece of the puzzle to the fascinating history of progressive rock music.

# Introduction

In the minds of most music critics, the idea of having a book devoted to fifty of the most influential progressive rock bands, must be like picking up one of those joke books about "sex after 40" and as you flip through it you find all the pages are blank. Actually seeing fifty progressive rock bands described in the book must really confound them. After all, other than for a brief time in the late sixties and early seventies, progressive rock has been largely ignored and abused by the music critics.

We live in a time where so much that is old, is new again. Yet it's puzzling how the media are so quick to selectively jump on revivals. If you're into space-rock, psychedelic music, retro-garage, or any one of a number of other revivals, you're able to find literally dozens of magazine articles that not only speak reverentially about the originators of those particular genres, but also of those following in their footsteps.

Not so with progressive rock. If the genre's acknowledged at all it's usually with a short article, which in most cases will be full of either left-handed compliments, sarcasm, or, in some cases, worse. It's quite easy to find music publications with huge portions devoted to one genre or another, except progressive rock. That gets a small line at the bottom left corner of the cover and the article itself will very likely use terms like "retrogressive" when referring to many of the new prog bands, all the while selectively ignoring how derivative so much current rock music is today.

One of the reasons for this, I believe, is that so many of the other genres tend to have strong visual or lifestyle elements. Take psychedelic for example; there are the posters, the light shows, the drugs and, of course, the fashions. The music is just one part of the mix. Take Heavy Metal as another example; there are currently dozens of magazines devoted to this genre and virtually all of them are full of the leather clad, posing and sneering characters we've come to associate with the music. It's more stance than substance in some cases. Whenever the media have focused on music of the seventies, it's always been Elton John and his big glasses and boots, or Glam-rock with it's makeup, sequins and stretchy skin tight outfits, or, on the other side, the down home folksy jeans-and-leather look of the Allman Brothers or the Eagles.

This gets to the heart of one of the major reasons why progressive rock is ignored. It's simply not about the clothes, or fashion or even lifestyle. Progressive rock has always been about the music. Keep in mind that many prog bands didn't even put their faces on the album covers. That space was generally reserved for some form of visual interpretation of the music inside. What they wore was nowhere near as important as the music they wrote. Dancing about on stage was nowhere near as important as how well they played. And in that regard if you weren't interested in investing time to actively listen and even read the lyrics, it didn't make good background music. Progressive rock required your attention and I'll say it again — progressive rock has always been about the music.

There were many who contacted me regarding my previous book, *The Progressive Rock Files*, expressing their appreciation at finding a book that wrote positively about the genre. There were a few however who took issue with the lack of what they called "critical analyses". I thought a few words here about this might be appropriate. First let me say that I've been in the broadcast industry for almost 30 years and over that time have been involved in many reviewer / critic-type programs, and never once did I hesitate to share my thoughts about a book, a movie, a TV program or a music release. That being said, I've always tried to look at an artistic endeavour from the more 'positive' side of things, and that's my approach once again with this project.

Further to this, I don't believe that "critical analyses" has ever served the artist. I don't believe it's ever made a painter paint a better picture, a poet write a better poem, or musician create a better piece of music. I tend to feel that "critical analyses" only serves those who write about it, and those few who read about it. And that's my objection to using that approach in my narrative. I've done this because, as I've indicated, I'm not at all convinced that saying something critical would in any way serve the purpose of promoting the genre. It's not because I think it's all perfect, or that I think it's flawless, it's just that it wasn't my intent to take that path. In all of this I'm reminded of the old saw: "Them that do, do; them that can't do, teach; and them that can't teach criticize." I've always felt that if someone was able to criticize a movie, book or piece of music he should also be able to go out and do it. Create, don't criticize.

This book, like the others in the series, showcases the most influential rock bands in the genre. As with any list, these influential bands may not be universally accepted as "the list", and I'm sure there'll be readers who question the inclusion of some bands and the exclusion of others. Such are the perils of trying to create a list. Still, when it came down to picking fifty, I made the list, checked it twice, and set about telling their stories. The selection of some bands was easy. The "big six" of Yes, Genesis, Emerson Lake & Palmer, Pink Floyd, King Crimson and Jethro Tull are a sure bet. Then you get into the other groups that have a high recognition factor — bands that many people have heard of — like Kansas, Focus, Procol Harum and of, course, The Moody Blues. But, ultimately, you get to a point where some of the most influential are not all that familiar. Take for example the "big three" Italian bands of Banco, PFM and Le Orme; or American's Happy The Man. You'll also find a mixture of the older bands and the new groups who are very much leading the progressive rock genre into the next century. Bands like Spock's Beard, Cast, IQ and The Flower Kings are all fine examples in this regard.

It's worth clarifying that the concept of "most influential" can mean a number of things. In some cases it's obvious. You have a number of bands who are constantly used as a reference point; bands like any of the "big six", or Camel or Renaissance. Any groups who have inspired others so profoundly deserve to be included. Others, however, are influential for other reasons — instrumentation, singing style or perhaps just the band's dogged determination to succeed. And there are some here who are responsible for creating whole new sub-genres of progressive rock like RIO and Zeuhl.

I hope that all of your favourites are in here, but I'm sure some will be missing. The bottom line is that if you had at least one album from each of the bands included in this list you would have one of the most comprehensive progressive rock record collections available. Each of the bands on this list has made a contribution to the genre that deserves to be recognized. These artists are shining examples of the great diversity, imagination and creativity that is progressive rock.

# ~ 1 ~
# Amon Duul II (Germany)

The first version of Amon Duul took shape in mid-1967 as a politically oriented avant-garde group of musicians whose prime directive was to experiment with drugs, music and politics. Out of this musical collective came Chris Karrer (guitar), who chose to focus more on the music. He joined up with John Weinzierl (guitar, bass) and Peter Leopold (drums) both originally from Amon Duul, then added Renate Knaup (vocals) Falk Rogner (organ, synth) and Dave Anderson (bass.) This lineup formed the core of Amon Duul II through much of the early 70's.

Their first couple albums, PHALLUS DEI and YETI, showed them searching for a style and still somewhat influenced by their earlier efforts. You can hear the beginnings of their space-influenced "krautrock" stylings albeit in a somewhat amateur manner. YETI displays a vast improvement over the first album, in large part because of the classic twenty four minute title track. In many respects these two releases have come to define space-rock.

Everything seems to have come together for their next release DANCE OF THE LEMMINGS (TANZ DER LEMMINGE) in 1971. By this time both Karrer and Weinzierl were writing more involved compositions with more complicated arrangements and adding these progressive rock elements to their brand of psychedelic space-rock. With influences such as Pink Floyd, the compositions became more elaborate, incorporating layer upon layer of electric and acoustic guitars mixed against a backdrop of organ, Mellotron and a variety of electronics. By 1972, the psychedelic elements had all but disappeared as Amon Duul II moved toward shorter compositions that favoured more of a song format, rather than the long rambling, spacey early compositions. Vocals became stronger and CARNIVAL IN BABYLON displayed this new approach admirably. The only improvised piece on the album was the nine minute closer *Hawknose Harlequin*. Amon Duul II's goal was always to focus on the music, and they were clearly attempting to move forward and distance themselves from their psychedelic roots.

The next release, WOLF CITY, emphasized the point. While still song-based, with shorter compositions, this album is a vibrant statement for the period. To document the time more fully a live concert was recorded and released as LIVE IN LONDON. The mid-70's saw Amon Duul II continuing to refine their musical style with the creation the masterful concept double album MADE IN GERMANY. Following that release the band, influenced by the beat-heavy music of the disco years, took their music to a more commercial level. Vocalist Knaup left the band, founders Karrer and Weinzierl hardly seemed to be making an effort, and Stephen Zauner (keyboards) and Klaus Ebert (bass) took centre stage more often as far as composition was concerned.

The albums of the late-70's all contain some fine tracks, but are not necessarily the recordings most sought after. In 1978, following the release of ONLY HUMAN, Weinzierl left the group. The band's future seemed in trouble. In an effort to breath life into Amon Duul II Karrer initiated a reunion, but the album that resulted, VORTEX, disappointed many fans and the band called it quits a second time. In the meantime John Weinzierl had gone to England and met up with original bassist Dave Anderson. Together they created a couple of releases under the Amon Duul name, which attempted a slight return to the band's original psychedelic roots, but with the incorporation of all the modern synths of the early-80s featured in so many of the techno-synth bands of the times. These releases were HAWK MEETS PENGUIN and MEETING WITH MEN MACHINES.

Nothing was heard from Amon Duul II for another five years — until 1987 to be exact — when the British version of the band released DIE LOSUNG at a time when Britain was going through a major psychedelic revival. This release put the Amon Duul II name at the top of the space-rock field for the day. The return of Amon Duul II in Germany came in 1993 with most of the original members fronted by Karrer. The music took yet another turn, more towards a synth-heavy techno-krautrock. While the compositions are similar to those of the mid-70's period, the production and instrumentation is very much 90's. Most recently, in 1997, Amon Duul II reinterpreted a number of their earlier classic tunes on an album called, of all things, FLAWLESS. At last word the band was still very active and working on new material to take the Amon Duul II name into the next millennium.

As with many of the bands listed here, Amon Duul II is included as one of the most influential prog rock bands because of the legacy of the music they've created. They've not always been innovators, but they've inspired others in Germany to create progressive rock, and for that they're noted here.

- o PHALLUS DEI (1969 Liberty)
- o YETI (1970 Liberty)
- o DANCE OF THE LEMMINGS (1971 UA)
- o CARNIVAL IN BABYLON (1972 UA)
- o WOLF CITY (1972 UA)
- o VIVE LA TRANCE (1973 UA)
- o LIVE IN LONDON (1974 UA)
- o HIJACK (1974 Nova)
- o LEMMINGMANIA (1975 UA Compilation)
- o MADE IN GERMANY (1975 Nova)
- o PYRAGONY X (1976 Nova)
- o ALMOST ALIVE (1977 Nova)
- o ONLY HUMAN (1978 Straud)

o VORTEX (1981)
o HAWK MEETS PENGUIN (1983 Illuminated)
o MEETING WITH MEN MACHINES (1982 Illuminated)
o AIRS ON A SHOESTRING (1987 Compilation)
o DIE LOSUNG (1989)
o FOOL MOON (1990)
o BBC LIVE IN CONCERT — 1973 (1992)
o SURROUNDED BY THE BARS (1993 Compilation)
o NADA MOONSHINE (1995)
o ETERNAL FLASHBACK (1995 Remixes)
o KOBE [RECONSTRUCTION'S] (1995 Remixes)
o LIVE IN TOKYO (1996)
o BEST OF 1969-1974 (1997 Compilation)
o FLAWLESS (1997 Re-recordings)

# ~ 2 ~
# Ange (France)

Ange were without question the most popular, innovative and influential French symphonic prog band of the 70's. Formed by brothers Christian DeCamps (lead vocals & keyboards) and Francis DeCamps (keyboards), they related to their audience by incorporating many patriotic idioms, French stories, slang, cultural references, and even issues of everyday French life. They were the prototypical French band and, as might be expected, were influenced by the politics of the day. It's been said that, in many ways, Ange typified all that was French in the same way that the Beach Boys typified the American Surf mentality.

Ange made their performance debut in March of 1970 and made a big impression with the media. The quick rise to prominence and touring took its toll on some of the members and they soon needed to replace their drummer and bass player. These holes were filled by Gerard Jelsch (drums) and Daniel Haas (bass), as well as adding Jean-Michel Brezovar on flute and guitar.

By the end of their first year together they had signed with Phonogram in France. The band's first release was CARICATURES, which came out two years after their formation, and it's a solid recording bearing many of the Ange trademarks, albeit in an early, perhaps more rudimentary, form — in particular the organ and Mellotron. Already noticeable was Christian DeCamp's poetic writing style and

unique and theatrical vocal delivery.

1973 saw Ange expand their fan base outside of France with the release LE CIETIERE DES ARLEQUINS. While it wasn't a huge change from their first album, the band displayed a little more self confidence in their musicianship and compositions. Later that year, Ange performed at the Reading Rock Festival to a huge standing ovation from a crowd of 30,000. However, while the audience in attendance may have witnessed progressive rock history, the fans at home missed out on any detailed reporting of the event because most of the French music journalists had slipped away at that point to get something to eat.

1974's AU DELA DU DELIRE was the last album with the original lineup, which is a shame since many consider this release to their best. Ange seemed to get all the elements together, from musicianship to composition, with this recording. Gerald Jelsch (drums) left to get off the non-stop touring treadmill and was replaced by Guenole Biger for the next LP, entitled EMILE JACOTEY. This was a concept LP featuring the voice of (presumably) the title character, and, from a song standpoint, the group were on a roll, even though this release was a little more upbeat even rockier to some degree. To many fans this album forms the junction between the early style and the band's later, more atmospheric work.

For the next LP, PAR LE FILS DU MANDRIN in 1976, Biger was replace on drums by Jean-Pierre Guichard and this was their biggest selling album to date. The music began to take on a more melancholy flavour with this recording and features subtle narration during the quieter moments of the music. To capitalize on their rising popularity they recorded an English version of the LP entitled FOR THE SONS OF MANDRIN. 1977 saw Ange cross the Atlantic for some rare North American concerts, specifically a half dozen performances in French speaking Quebec, Canada. Two double live albums, TOME VI and 1970/1971 EN CONCERT, were released which, to a great degree, captured the sound of Ange live and so both remain sound documents of the band;s energy on stage.

At the end of the 70's, Ange changed members again when Brezovar and Haas left to pursue solo careers. They were replaced by Claude Demet (guitar) and Gerald Renard (bass), and with this lineup Ange put out their last LP of the 70's, GUET APENS. This album displays a slightly more "spacey", almost Pink Floyd influenced approach. Most fans consider the band's last true "progressive rock" LP to be 1980's VU D'UN CHIEN which showcases a much more aggressive guitar style that was prevalent in the arena rock of the day.

Ange carried on with further lineup changes revolving around the brothers DeCamp, recording into the 80's, but sadly, not as a prog band. Albums such as FOU released in 1984 showed the band being content to compose in a shorter, pop or rock influenced style. And while the material had a pleasant sound with wonderful melodies, fans of Ange's prog style missed the old depth in the new material. They reformed in 1995 with the original lineup for one last tour which resulted in the double live CD UN PETIT TOUR ET PUIS S'EN VANT. Ange proved to be a powerful influence on many of their French contemporaries such as Atoll and Mona Lisa, as well as many of the modern prog bands who have followed in their musical footsteps.

o IN CONCERT (1971)
o CARICATURES (Philips 1972)
o LE CIMETIERE DES ARLEQUINS (Philips 1973)
o AU DELA DU DELIRE (Philips 1974)
o EMILE JACOTEY (Philips 1975)

o PAR LE FILS DE MANDRIN (Philips 1976)
o FOR THE SONS OF MANDRIN (English Version Philips 1976)
o TOME IV (Philips 1977)
o 1970/1971 EN CONCERT (1977 RCA)
o ANGE CHANTE SES PLUS GRANDS SUCCES (1977 Phillips)
o EN CONCERT (1978)
o GUET APENS (Philips 1978)
o VU D'UN CHIEN (Philips 1980)
o MOTEUR! (1981)
o A PROPOS DE (1982)
o LA GARE DE TROYES (1983)
o FOU (Trema 1984)
o UNPETIT TOUR ET PUIS S'EN VANT (1995)


~ **3** ~

# Anglagard (Sweden)

From the photo of the lone Mellotron standing resolutely in a forest glade that appears at the top of their web site (and inside their first album), you get the feeling that there's something a little different about the Swedish band Anglagard. More than any other instrument, the Mellotron has come to symbolize progressive rock music, and it was this instrument on which the music of Anglagard was centred. Their music included all that was good about the symphonic prog of the 70's and matched with the modern production qualities of the symphonic prog in the 90's. Critics hailed them as no neo-progressive band — these guys were the real thing.

Anglagard formed in Stockholm in 1991 by the meeting of Tord Lindman (guitar), Johan Hogberg (bass), Tomas Jonson (keyboards) and Jonas Engdegard (guitar.) All four shared a desire to create and perform music that incorporated the experimental and progressive spirit of the 70's. In early 1992 they added Mattias Olsson (drums) and Anna Holmgren (flute.)

Their first CD, HYBRIS, was recorded in the summer of 1992 and brought them international acclaim. It is considered by many to be one of the best albums of the progressive rock genre. The music is reminiscent of groups like King Crimson, Gentle Giant, Genesis and Shylock. Typically, their material is developed around longer compositions that are more musically based. They create compositions with many moods and many time and tempo changes. While response in Sweden was limited, the CD caught the ears of many in the United States; so much so that they were invited to perform at Progfest 93. Their performance was a resounding success and they were immediately invited to return the following year. Their blend of guitars, analog synths, Hammond organ, Mellotrons and flute proved to be the hit of the show. That event, plus a four-date return tour later in 1993, made them the darlings of the progressive rock scene. HYBRIS eventually went on to sell over 7,000 copies at a time where there was little if any mainstream prog distribution network and certainly no mainstream commercial or media attention. The LP was voted "Album of the Year" in a number of prog polls.

Even though the group had been together only a short time, musical differences began to form and rumours started to fly regarding their impending split. They agreed to stay together to complete their second CD, EPILOG, which was released in late 1994. Unlike their first LP, which contained some singing, Epilog was entirely instrumental and tended to be somewhat quieter and more introspective. It too was voted "Album of the Year" in prog polls. Anglagard split shortly after their return engagement at Progfest 94. A live recording of their Progfest performance was released called BURIED ALIVE in 1996.
Before the break up of Anglagard, there had been some talk of the original trio minus Tord working on a new project, but nothing has come of it. As of this writing, Johan, Anna and Tord were all in music school, while Tomas and Jonas were writing music and Mattias was playing in a commercial pop band.

Anglagard's music is nostalgic and yet the production maintains a very modern sound to the ear. Hailed by many as one of the best progressive rock groups of the 90's, Anglagard may be credited with inspiring a disproportionate number of prog groups to emerge from Sweden. They also demonstrated that it was possible to create intense, complicated symphonic prog that was also entertaining.

- o HYBRIS (1992 Mellotronen)
- o EPILOG (1994 HYB)
- o BURIED ALIVE (1996)

# ~ **4** ~

# Banco (Italy)

Their full name, Banco Del Mutuo Soccorso, in English means The Bank of Mutual Trust.

With their dual keyboards and operatic vocals, Banco is one of the finest Italian progressive rock bands ever. The band's focus has always been very classically oriented piano with keyboard solos, but they were always able to rock out much the same way PFM might. They formed in Rome in 1971 when members of two top Italian bands Fiori Di Campo and Experience decided to join forces. Vittorio Nocenzi (keyboards) and Gianni Nocenzi (keyboards), who'd recorded some material on an Italian pop compilation in the late 60's, joined up with Marcello Todaro (guitar), Francesco Di Giacomo (vocals), Renato D'Angelo (bass) and Pierluigi Calderoni (drums.)

First on the agenda was a change in musical direction. They dispensed with the shorter pop styled songs and focused on longer more complex compositions that took full advantage of Vittorio's love of classical music. Banco released their first LP BANCO DEL MUTUO SOCCORSO in early 1972, which turned out to be a landmark release in the world of Italian progressive rock. Musically it was full of atmosphere, instrumental drama and poetic lyrics. Not only did the music highlight all the progressive hallmarks of arranging and composition, it also featured a moneybox-shaped cover which even had a coin slot with a strip of band photos coming out of it. A few months later the band was back in the studio recording their follow-up album, a musical concept based on Charles Darwin's theory of evolution entitled DARWIN! Following this release came the first lineup change when Rodolfo Maltese from the band Homo Sapiens replaced Marcello Todaro on guitars.

The following year, Banco released IO SONO NATO LIBERO, which continued to develop their musical style. After its release the band found themselves without a record deal. Given their high profile outside of Italy, they were quickly singed by Emerson Lake & Palmer's Manticore label, joining countrymen PFM. Banco's first release on Manticore simply, called BANCO, was a collection of older songs with new English lyrics. This was followed by a landmark live show in Venice with Keith Emerson in the audience. The band's popularity was soaring at this point.

In 1976 Banco released two recordings: the first, GARAFANO ROSSO, was a movie soundtrack; the second was more a continuation of the traditional Banco style entitled COME IN UN'ULTIMA CENA, or in English AS IN A LAST SUPPER. The record was released in both languages and was followed by a European tour supporting Gentle Giant. After a year without a record Banco hit the racks with what is probably their most complex recording, DI TERRA, in 1978. This totally instrumental release showcased the band playing along with the full orchestra Dell 'Unione Musicisti di Roma, and shows them performing at their peak with equal parts classical, jazz and even some rock. The following year, Banco released CANTO DI PRIMAVERA showing a return to the more traditional material with eight new compositions, all with vocals and slightly shorter in length.

As they moved into the 80's this approach of shorter, simpler, song-based compositions became even more prominent. For many, the live album CAPOLINEA, in 1980 and featuring some of the band's earlier, longer material, signaled the end of an era. The group officially shortened their name to just Banco in 1980 and through much of the 80's kept up their usual hectic pace releasing a series of LP's which all featured shorter songs aimed at the singles market and radio. From 1986 through 1989 there was no new Banco material. Musically members kept busy in various aspects of the music business.

As the 90's dawned, the group reunited and returned to their original name Banco Del Mutuo Soccorso. Their new live shows even included a number of compositions from their early progressive rock albums. In an effort to return to their glory days, Banco's first release of the 90's, DA QUI MESSERE SI DOMINA LA VALLE, featured new versions of material from their first two albums. This project fueled their creative fires and gave members a renewed enthusiasm to pursue the more complex material they'd left behind. The next release, IL 13, came in 1994 and, while not a return to the past, it certainly is a stronger blend of the old complexity and the new mood of the band. Following an intensive tour of Japan, Banco released NUDO in 1997 showcasing "unplugged" versions of tunes from their glory days. Twenty five years later Banco is still very much alive and well. A rich catalogue of musical recordings spanning more than two decades assures their place as one of the most influential progressive rock bands.

- BANCO DEL MUTUO SOCCORSO (1972 Ricordi)
- DARWIN (1972 Ricordi)
- IO SONO NATO LIBERO (1973 Ricordi)
- BANCO (1975 Manticore)
- GAROFANO ROSSO (1976 Manticore)
- COME IN UN'ULTIMA CENA [AS IN A LAST SUPPER] (1976 Manticore)
- ...DI TERRA (1978 Ricordi)
- CANTO DI PRIMAVERA (1979 Ricordi)
- CAMPOLINEA (1980 Ricordi)
- URGENTISSIMO (1980 CBS)

- BUONE NOTIZIE (1981 CBS)
- BANCO (1983 CBS)
- ...E VIA (1985 CBS)
- DONNA PLAUTILLA (1989 Raro Records)
- DA QUI MESSERE SI DOMINA LA VALLE (91 Virgin)
- LA STORIA (1993 Virgin)
- I GRANDI SUCCESSI (1993 Columbia/Sony)
- IL 13 (1994 EMI Records)
- LE ORIGINI (1996 BMG/Ricordi)
- ANTOLOGIA (1996 Disky Communications/EMI)
- NUDO (1997 KingRecord/EMI)
- PAPAGAYO CLUB 1972 (1998 Prehistoric)
- BANCO DEL MUTUO SOCCORSO LIVE 1970 (1998 Mellow)

~ **5** ~

# Camel (England)

The members of Camel all came out of an R&B environment to form in 1972. The band was made up of Peter Bardens (keyboard), Andy Latimer (guitar), Doug Ferguson (bass) and Andy Ward (drums.) Bardens had spent time with a variety of outfits like Shotgun Express, Village and, most notably, Them, Van Morrison's outfit, before joining up with Latimer, Ward and Ferguson who were then in a band called Brew.

Camel's first album was released in 1973 and was followed with an annual release throughout the 70's. Their first two recordings — CAMEL in 1973 and MIRAGE in 1974 — displayed Camel's penchant for melodic compositions featuring long instrumental excursions. In 1975 they released THE SNOW GOOSE, a musical interpretation of the book authored by Paul Gallico. The band felt that their musical vision was an accurate representation of the book, however the author had a different idea. To make matters worse, he hadn't been consulted about the use of his work in another context. He filed a law suit against Camel, which resulted in their record company being forced to publish an apology for the fact that no formal permission had been sought before using the material. All the publicity didn't hurt and Camel went on to win Melody Maker's "Brightest Hope" award for 1975.

By the time of their fifth release, RAINDANCES in 1977, the band had matured as a performing unit but, symptomatic of the times, their compositions began to

tighten up and become somewhat more mainstream. They also had the assistance of Caravan co-founder Richard Sinclair and Mel Collins on woodwinds which added a new element to their sound. In 1979 Bardens departed and Camel acquired Kit Watkins, formerly of Happy The Man, as keyboardist. The album that resulted, I CAN SEE YOUR HOUSE FROM HERE, is not usually considered their best work, but it was certainly the one that got the most attention in America, in part because of Watkins involvement.

When THE SINGLE FACTOR was released in 1982, many wondered if Camel had sold out, since it was an album full of shorter compositions. Latimer by now was the sole surviving constant of Camel but he pulled out all the stops when it came to the musical supporting cast. THE SINGLE FACTOR saw the return of Peter Bardens on keyboards assisted by such notables as Anthony Phillips, Chris Rainbow, Francis Monkman, Dave Mattacks, David Paton, Simon Phillips and a host of others. The attempt at singles failed and Latimer regrouped with the 1984 release of THE STATIONARY TRAVELLER. Latimer was still working within the shorter song context, but the album contained no less than four instrumentals. Once again he was assisted by many notable musicians including Paul Burgess, David Paton, Chris Rainbow and Ton Scherpenzeel from Kayak.

After this release Camel ceased recording and instead focused more on live performances. It wasn't until 1991 that a new Camel release was found on the shelves: it was DUST AND DREAMS. Picking up where THE SNOW GOOSE and NUDE left off, this too was a concept LP based on Steinbeck's *The Grapes of Wrath*. Gone were the attempts at singles as Camel returned to a more lush and symphonic approach with each character employing a musical theme throughout. After many years on major labels, Latimer chose to produce, package and distribute DUST AND DREAMS on his own, an indication of where progressive rock was at in the early nineties. Latimer then released a series of live CDs capturing the stage efforts of Camel in each of the three decades of their existence. Then in 1996 Camel returned with yet another concept CD, this one focusing on the Irish potato famine and exodus entitled HARBOUR OF TEARS. A somewhat more subdued musical experience, the recording dealt with a troubling time in Irish history and Latimer attempts to capture those sentiments in his compositions.

Camel, like some of the others mentioned, have achieved the 'status-of-description', whereby new progressive rock artists' material is described as sounding like them. Unfortunately the band never achieved superstardom like many of their contemporaries. This wasn't because of a lack of musicianship or compositional skills, because their material was as good as some and better than others. If anything, Camel's weak point was simply their nondescript nature. There was no individual out front like Ian Anderson or Peter Gabriel. If Camel suffered from anything it was lack of image. Fortunately what they lacked in terms of image was made up for in musicianship and Camel continue to build on their substantial musical catalogue of high quality progressive rock.

o CAMEL (1973 MCA)
o MIRAGE (1974 Janus)
o THE SNOW GOOSE (1975 Janus)
o MOONMADNESS (1976 Janus)
o RAIN DANCES (1977 London)
o A LIVE RECORD (1978 London)
o BREATHLESS (1978 London)
o I CAN SEE YOUR HOUSE FROM HERE (1979 London)
o NUDE (1981 London)
o THE SINGLE FACTOR (1982 Passport)
o STATIONARY TRAVELLER (1984 Decca)
o PRESSURE POINTS LIVE (1984 Decca)
o ECHOES (1991 Polygram)

o DUST AND DREAMS (1992 Camel)
o ON THE ROAD 1972 (1993)
o ON THE ROAD 1982 (1994)
o NEVER LET GO [LIVE] (1994)
o HARBOUR OF TEARS (1996)

# ~ 6 ~
# Can (Germany)

Can was formed in Cologne, Germany in 1968. They proved to be an inspiration for any band wondering how far they could stretch the progressive rock genre. The emphasis here is more progressive than it is rock. In many respects Can was always a few steps ahead of everyone else. If you were into early Frank Zappa, Velvet Underground and others of that ilk you were probably listening to Can. Can along with Tangerine Dream are considered by many to be the most influential modern progressive German bands and, interestingly enough, both got involved with film soundtrack composition.

Their first independently released album, MONSTER MOVIE, came out in 1969 featuring an already burgeoning fountain of non-rock influences from stream of consciousness lyrics to tribal percussion. Personnel changes resulted in original members Malcolm Mooney and American David Johnson departing. Mooney was replaced by street singer Damo Suzuki. Can's musical style consisted of sparse arrangements, simple harmonies and highly repetitive rhythms making for a kind of hypnotic improvisation. In addition, they incorporated many classical and avant-garde influences into a style that came to full bloom with their third release, TAGO MAGO, in 1971.

Many consider the band to have peaked with their 1973 release FUTURE DAYS. Shortly after this Suzuki left and the idea of having a dedicated vocalist was seen as a dead end, so everyone in the group took up the vocal challenge. Can eventually solidified into a group consisting of Michael Karoli (guitar, vocals), Holger Czukay (bass, vocals), Jaki Liebezeit (percussion, wind instruments) and Irman Schmidt (keyboards, vocals.) Both Czukay and Schmidt studied under Karlheinz Stockhausen and the modern 20th Century compositional traits are evident.

At the end of 1976 they even managed to achieve the unthinkable by having a top thirty hit single in the UK entitled *I Want More*. Where some bands may have

used that success to move into more of a singles direction, Can remained true to their art. In 1977 new members Rosko Gee (bass) and Reebop Kwaku Bah (percussion) were added to the lineup, while Czukay changed direction and focused on electronics and tape loops.

Never having achieved more than cult status with a group of loyal fans, the band split in 1978. Still, their musical influence can be heard in bands such as Public Image Limited, Einsturzende Neubauten and others. Their music has less in common with rock than it does with 20<sup>th</sup> Century Classical composition. Instead of recording short concise pop songs, Can experimented with electronic music, non-traditional music, noise and everything else they could cram into the studio. They created an aggressive, dissonant style of music, that continues to prove

*Can*

rewarding for those looking to challenge their listening repertoire.

- o MONSTER MOVIE (1969 Spoon)
- o SOUNDTRACKS (1970 Restless)
- o TAGO MAGO (1971 Restless)
- o EGE BAMYASI (1972 Restless)
- o FUTURE DAYS (1973 Spoon)
- o LIMITED EDITION (1974 United Artists)
- o SOON OVER BABALUMA (1974 Enigma)
- o LANDED (1975 Mute)
- o OPENER (1976 Sunset Compilation)
- o UNLIMITED EDITION (1976 Mute)
- o FLOW MOTION (1976 Mute)
- o SAW DELIGHT (1977 Mute)
- o OUT OF REACH (1978 Harvest)
- o CAN (1979 Mute)
- o CANNIBALISMS (1978 United Artists)
- o CANNIBALISM 1 (1980 Spoon)
- o DELAY...1968 (1981 Spoon)
- o INCANDESCENCE (1981 Virgin)
- o TIME RITE (1989 Fink & Star)
- o CANNIBALISM 2 (1990 Mute)
- o CANNIBALISM 3 (1990 Mute)

# ~ 7 ~
# Caravan (England)

Caravan is one of the more successful bands that sprang out of the highly creative Canterbury, Kent, England scene of the late 60's and early 70's. And while many of the other bands took a more avant-garde or jazzy approach, Caravan tended to create music that was closer to the prog mainstream, if you want to call it that. Their history, as with a number of Canterbury bands, begins with The Wild Flowers — a group that first took shape as far back as 1964. Out of this group Caravan formed in 1968.

The original lineup consisted of Richard Sinclair (bass, vocals), David Sinclair (keyboards), Pye Hastings (guitar, vocals), and Richard Coughlan (drums) and it was this lineup that produced their first three recordings between 1968 and

1971. While the first self-titled LP contained compositions of a more "pop" nature, with a bit of psychedelia thrown in, many critics feel the best of the trio was the second which has the unwieldy title IF I COULD DO IT AGAIN I WOULD DO IT ALL OVER YOU.

As was typical of the Canterbury bands, they achieved much critical success for their efforts but popular success eluded them. David Sinclair left in late 1971 and he went on to yet another Canterbury outfit called Matching Mole which was a more jazz oriented group. His replacement was Steve Miller (keyboards) and the band went on to record the 1972 release WATERLOO LILY. This LP showed a marked step towards a jazzier style, influenced greatly by Miller's piano work. However, not long after this Richard Sinclair and Miller joined up with Phil Miller and Pip Pyle which eventually led to the formation of Hatfield and The North. David Sinclair, who had appeared as a guest on the tour in support of WATERLOO LILY, felt so comfortable with Caravan's new lineup of John G. Perry, Hastings and Coughlan that he decided to stay.

In 1973 Caravan was asked to do a special one-nighter at London's Dury Lane Theatre with backing from a small classical orchestra, the results of which were released on CARAVAN AND THE NEW SYMPHONIA in 1974. Just before the release of the album Perry left and was replaced by Mike Wedgewood (previously with Curved Air.) With this lineup they entered the studio and came out with CUNNING STUNTS in 1975 which fans considered to be their best work since IN THE LAND OF GREY AND PINK. CUNNING STUNTS was an album of great melodies, strong vocal performances and some of their most complex musicianship. David Sinclair decided once again to leave to pursue a solo career, which in the long run came to nothing. His replacement was Jan Schelhaas, a more than competent keyboard player. Dek Messacar was brought in to replace Mike Wedgewood in early 1977, and it was with the lineup of Hastings, Coughlan, Messecar and Shelhaas that the band recorded BETTER BY FAR in 1977. The album was a modern blend of old and new — some very catchy pop tunes with a couple of longer more adventurous tracks. However, lackluster sales caused the group to rethink their direction. In the meantime they took time off and got involved in other musical projects.

Then in 1979 Caravan reformed with the same lineup minus David Sinclair and released THE ALBUM showing their musical direction picking up where they had left off. Nothing new was ventured, just a continuation of a comfortable musical direction. More tours were undertaken and then another album, BACK TO FRONT, was released.

The 80's saw sporadic gigs, which included a couple appearances at the Marquee Club in 1983 and a performance at the Canterbury Festival in 1985, then nothing

until 1990 when the band was asked to reform and perform for a TV show. Their performance consisted of material mostly from their early recordings. They continued to perform for the next few years, touring in England and Europe, however, the constant grind finally got to Pye Hastings who tired of performing only old material. He retreated to a studio to work on solo projects. Around this time Richard Sinclair was concentrating on his solo work under the name Caravan of Dreams. Eventually Hastings dropped his solo projects and decided to record a Caravan album instead. In late 1994 Hastings, David Sinclair and Jimmy Hastings joined up with Geoff Richardson, Richard Coughlan and bassist Jimmy Leverton to record THE BATTLE OF HASTINGS released in 1995. It turned out to be a fine collection of compositions, very much carrying the Caravan trademark, with a nice blend of organ, violin, flute, sax and Pye's vocals.

While many of the other mainstream bands were accused of self indulgence, Caravan was seen to be a more sincere progressive rock band. Perhaps it was because of their Canterburian connection. True to the Canterburian form, their material was jaunty, upbeat, and even somewhat humorous in tone, all with the ever-present jazzy feel. Caravan, with it's still changing lineup of members, continues to record and tour much to the delight of a small but dedicated following.

o CARAVAN (1968 MGM)
o IF I COULD DO IT ALL OVER AGAIN, I'D DO IT ALL OVER YOU (1970 Decca)
o IN THE LAND OF GREY AND PINK (1971 Deram)
o WATERLOO LILY (1972 Deram)
o FOR GIRLS WHO GROW PLUMP IN THE NIGHT (1973 Deram)
o CARAVAN AND THE NEW SYMPHONIA (1974 Deram)
o CUNNING STUNTS (1975 Decca)
o BLIND DOG AT ST. DUSTANS (1976 Arista)
o CANTERBURY TALES (1976 Decca)
o BETTER BY FAR (1977 Arista)
o THE ALBUM (1980 Kingdom)
o THE BEST OF CARAVAN LIVE (1980 Kingdom)
o THE SHOW OF OUR LIVES (1981 Decca)
o BACK TO FRONT (1982 Kingdom)
o THE CANTERBURY COLLECTION (1984 Kingdom)
o THE BEST OF CARAVAN (1987 London)
o LOOKING BACK (1988 Disky BV)
o SONGS AND SIGNS (1991 Elite)
o BBC LIVE IN CONCERT (1991 Windsong)
o WITH AN EAR TO THE GROUND (1991 Windsong)
o LIVE '93 (1993 Demon/Code90)
o COOL WATER (1994 HTD)
o CANTERBURY TALES — THE BEST OF CARAVAN (1994 Deram)
o THE BATTLE OF HASTINGS (1995 HTD)
o ALL OVER YOU (1996 HDT)
o CANTERBURY COMES TO LONDON / LIVE FROM THE ASTORIA (1997 HDT)
o SONGS FOR OBLIVIAN FISHERMEN (1998 Hux Records)
o ETHER WAY (1998 Hux Records)

# ~ 8 ~

# Cast (Mexico)

Cast is included in this stellar lineup not only because of their musical accomplishments, but also because they embody the persistence required to make it in the world of progressive rock. They've struggled and are prog survivors. Cast has been around since 1978 and, up until the early 90's, really seemed to be performing only for their own enjoyment; for the love of the music. They are an inspiration for so many young up-and-coming prog bands.

The lineup has been constant from the beginning with core members Francisco Hernandez (guitar), Rodolfo Gonzalez (bass), and Alfonso Vidales (keyboards.) In 1993 Dino Brassea joined on vocals along with Jose Caire on percussion. Other members over the years have included Enrique Slim (percussion), Javier Rosales (guitar) and Marcos Castro (guitar.)

Cast built their own recording studio, called appropriately Cast Studio, in 1992 in Alfonso Vidales home, which is what precipitated their prolific output. Cast has created eight studio albums since 1993. Their first major exposure to the prog world was the 1995 edition of Progfest in Los Angeles. Since then they've performed in other parts of the U.S. (ProgDay), Argentina (Asociacion del Rock Progresivo), Quebec City Canada (ProgEst) and even Europe. In an effort to promote the progressive rock genre, Cast has even created and staged three highly successful prog festivals, called Baja Prog, in their home country of Mexico. These extremely well run events have been nothing short of first class affairs featuring international lineups of some of the top prog bands of the day.

While all of the members have full time jobs or own their own businesses, they still make time, to create, record and perform some of the best neo-progressive rock today. Given that Vidales' parents are classically trained musicians, its easy to see why Cast's epic style has roots in similarly arranged classical music. In the early 80's Cast found time to record material but didn't release it on CD. Many of these compositions were fine tuned and included on their CD releases in the 90's. So, while their first CD, LANDING IN A SERIOUS MIND, contained material strictly from 1994, their second release, SOUNDS OF IMAGINATION, has a blend of older material from 1985 with the new compositions from 1994. The release THIRD CALL featured new material from 1994 with some selections from 1989. It wasn't until FOUR ACES, their fourth CD, that much of their early material was eventually released.

As some have noted, their earlier music borrows from mid-period Genesis, namely TRICK OF THE TAIL and WIND AND WUTHERING. Over the years, however, the band has firmly established its own style, and they used that inspiration as a stepping stone to crafting their own musical sensibility. In many cases their music has become infinitely more complex than their inspiration, especially their releases ENDLESS SIGNS, BEYOND REALITY and ANGELS AND DEMONS. These recording are full of longer compositions — some as long as 20 minutes — with plenty of dynamics and musical twists and turns, and all going from very pastoral flute work to the grand epic keyboard signatures. And with each recording the sound quality has improved by leaps and bounds.

Within the prog community there has been a long running debate over whether or not artists should sing in their native language. Some do and some don't. For Cast it's always been easy to decide. From the beginning their material has virtually always been sung in English. The group maintains that progressive rock simply sounds better sung in English. Lyrically, much, if not all, of their material targets a more philosophical, even spiritual content. It's not unusual for the lyrics to focus on the blessings we have in this life or the work of Angels here on earth.

Cast is one of those bands that seem to embody all that progressive rock represents. Whether it be determination to be true to your musical aspirations, to stick to your dreams, or to work hard and to give back to the prog community, Cast does it all, and they're an inspiration for any up-and-coming proggers. In the late 90's both Vidales and guitarist Hernandez took time out to develop their solo careers. Vidales has released two solo CDs entitled ENTRE DOS PAREDES (1995) and CLAVICO (1998), while Hernandez released WHISPERS FROM THE WIND (1997.)

- LANDING IN A SERIOUS MIND (1994 Independent)
- SOUNDS OF IMAGINATION (1994 Independent)
- THIRD CALL (1994 Independent)
- FOUR ACES (1995 Independent)
- ENDLESS SIGNS (1995 Independent)
- BEYOND REALITY (1996 Independent)
- A VIEW OF CAST LIVE (1997 Independent)
- ANGELS AND DEMONS (1997 Independent)
- A LIVE EXPERIENCE (1999 Musea)
- IMAGINARY WINDOW (1999 Musea)

# ~ 9 ~
# Deus Ex Machina (Italy)

More than any band, Deus Ex Machina became the darlings of the prog community in the early 90's. For many, they epitomized everything that was brilliant about Italian progressive rock in the 70's but with all the modern production sensibilities. Critics every where hailed them as spectacular.

Deus Ex Machina formed in 1985 in Bologna, Italy. After some initial personnel changes the lineup consisted of Alberto Piras (vocals), Maurino Collina (guitar),

Luigi Ricciardello (keyboards), Alessandro Bonetti (violin), Alessandro Porrece (bass) and Marco Matteuzzi (drums.) Their musical style and especially vocals have consistently drawn almost mythical comparisons to Area and vocalist Demetrio Stratos. Vocalist Alberto Piras uses his voice in much the same way — a very emotional roller coaster delivery, treating the voice as another instrument in the compositional mix.

Their first official effort together was a rock opera based on the struggle between man and nature — prog material for sure. It was staged in 1990 to positive critical response. As has happened many times over the years with adventurous projects such as this, finances proved to be it's undoing. The cost of mounting such an extravagant production far exceeded the band's ability to make it profitable. Their music was described as "unusual" and "extremely elaborate". Overall, there was the distinctive blend of rock with classical and jazz. Added to the mix was the band's decision to write and perform lyrics in Latin.

Deus Ex Machine headed into the studio in May of 1990 for two days of recording. In 1991 the rock opera GLADIUM CAELI was released, "warts" and all. Late 1991 saw the first personnel shuffle with the arrival of drummer Claudio Trotta. The new drummer and the band's quest for musical evolution resulted in the second CD being titled after the band. It was recorded between September of 1991 and July 1992 and even through it was a musical departure from their rock opera it was still received well by the critics.

In 1993 vocalist Alberto Piras began composing new material based on a book he authored dealing with the use of power and the dictatorship of mediocrity in modern society. The band went into the studio in the summer of 1994 to begin recording the new work. With more studio time at their disposal, they made full use of the facilities. The resulting album, DE REPUBLICA, was the group's third and was released early in 1995. It marked another evolutionary step in the band's musical style. This release, and the touring they undertook, helped to push Deus Ex Machina to the forefront of the then current crop of progressive rock artists. Not as overtly accessible as bands such as The Flower Kings or Spock's Beard, none-the-less Deus Ex Machina hold a special place in the hearts of fans of 70's prog as they endeavour to stay true to the form. DE REPUBLICA was voted "Best Album of the Year" by prog critics around the world. A defining moment for the band occurred with their performance at California's Progfest in 1995. Many in the audience were surprised at the tightness of the live set and the band won over more fans. Since then they've toured the U.S. twice, as well as performing at a progressive rock festival in Stockholm Sweden in the Fall of 1996. Deus Ex Machina released their fourth studio album, EQUILIBRISMO DA INSOFFERENZA, in 1998.

A group with roots in the older Italian sound — heavy keyboard and guitar arrangements spiced with violin form their foundation — this is full-fledged progressive rock with lots of odd time changes, complex arrangements and great musicianship on both long and short compositions. They are easily one of the fifty most influential progressive rock bands for their uncompromising compositional style and for how they've managed to resurrect the traditional Italian sound of prog in the 90's, influencing others such as America's A Triggering Myth and Italy's D.F.A. As outlined in numerous interviews and on the band's web site, Deus Ex Machina is proud of its trademark ethos which is best described as 'a permanent state of evolution.'

- o GLADIUM CAELI (1990 Kaliphonia)
- o DEUS EX MACHINA (1993 Kaliphonia)
- o DE REPUBLICA (1994 Kaliphonia)
- o DIACRONIE METRONOMICHE (1996 Kaliphonia)
- o EQUILIBRISMO DA INSOFFERENZA (1998 Kaliphonia)

# ~ 10 ~
# Dream Theater (United States)

A decade ago, the concept of putting progressive rock and heavy metal together might have seemed somewhat far fetched. However, in an age of specialization and engineering, anything seems possible; hence the relatively new sub-genre of prog-metal which came on the scene in the early 90's. Take the influences of bands such as Rush, Kansas and Queen; add some contemporary hard rock like Queensryche; and you begin to see where the bands in the prog-metal genre get their musical motivation.

At the forefront of the genre is Dream Theater. Originally they were known as Majesty consisting of John Petrucci (guitar), John Myung (bass), Mike Portnoy (drums) and Kevin Moore (keyboards.) All but Moore had attended the Berklee School of Music in Boston. Their debut recording, WHEN DREAM AND DAY UNITE in 1989, featured Charlie Dominici on vocals. Unfortunately, while the record was well received by a growing group of fans and some radio stations, sales were insufficient to keep the record company interested, so they dropped the band and shortly afterward Dominici was let go. Interestingly, he was called back for one final concert when Marillion specifically requested Dream Theater be the supporting act. They opened the show with a new track called *Metropolis*. The nine and half minute composition was a clear indication of the direction Dream Theater were heading. The band thought finding a replacement vocalist would be a snap, and yet it took almost two years to find the right person. During this time they performed the new material as instrumentals and took the opportunity to perfect their musical chops. They eventually recruited James Labrie on vocals and

released IMAGES AND WORDS in 1992. To their credit, the band was able to get an edited version of one track off the CD, entitled *Pull Me Under*, aired a number of times on the American music video channel MTV. It was enough to get them noticed, and gave them the incentive to carry on with their musical vision.

Their sound as defined on this recording was guitar and rhythm heavy, but not at the expense of keyboards. While keyboards may have played a secondary role in Dream Theater's lineup when compared to bands like Yes or Genesis, they were still very present and very influential to the overall sound. Longer compositions in the eight, nine and eleven minute range provided ample time for musical virtuosity, specially guitars and drums. There were lots of time and tempo changes in multi-part compositions packed with drama and yet, through it all, the band was able to rock.

Recognition for Dream Theater grew quickly everywhere, it seemed, except in the United States. The CD went Gold in Japan and a short tour was hastily arranged. Next came what the band labeled the "Music in Progress" tour of Europe. It was on this tour that they recorded the LIVE AT THE MARQUEE EP. By 1994 Dream Theater had started work on their third album. It was during this time that keyboardist Kevin Moore decided to leave the band over what were loosely called musical differences. His replacement turned out to be Derek Sherinian, another Berklee alumnus.

The album AWAKE was released worldwide in October and sold well. It debuted on the *Billboard* chart at No. 32 and sold over 40,000 copies in Germany. The band then toured worldwide in support of this release.

In 1995 Dream Theater recorded their 23 minute epic *A Change of Seasons* and packaged it up with some live material from Ronnie Scott's club in London for an EP entitled appropriately A CHANGE OF SEASONS. Through 1996 and 1997 the band again toured the world performing old songs with new arrangements and new material destined for their next studio release. That new material found it's way to CD in September of 1997 when FALLING INTO INFINITY was released.

After tours in support of the CD, in January of 1999, keyboardist Derek Sherinian announced his departure after four years with Dream Theater. His replacement was announced as Jordan Rudess, who once toured with the Dixie Dregs. Mike Portnoy and John Petrucci had worked with Rudess in the one-off Liquid Tension Experiment, and the experience appears to have left a positive impression. The band was quoted as saying that it was that experience which provided them the vision of where they saw Dream Theater in the 21st Century.

Dream Theater are included here because of their high profile, notoriety as individual musicians, and their determination at getting their music heard and seen. Dream Theater has been instrumental in pioneering a genre and taking their hard edged version of progressive rock to a whole new group of music fans.

- WHEN DREAM AND DAY UNITE (87 Mechanic)
- IMAGES AND WORDS (92 Atco)
- LIVE AT THE MARQUEE (1993 Warner Music)
- AWAKE (94 EastWest Records)
- A CHANGE OF SEASONS (95 EastWest Records)
- FALLING INTO INFINITY (97 EastWest Records)

# ~ 11 ~
# Echolyn (United States)

For some, progressive rock doesn't mean inaccessible. Echolyn's trademark multi-part harmonies and contrapuntal composition style is complicated and yet still very accessible, and all without sounding overtly commercial. To describe Echolyn you could say they are a blend of the vocal harmonies of Yes and the more challenging arrangements of Gentle Giant.

Formed in Philadelphia in late 1989, the band eventually came to consist of Chris Buzby (keyboards, vocals), Ray Weston (percussion, vocals), Brett Kull (guitars, vocals), Paul Ramsey (drums) and Tom Hyatt (bass, midi pedals.) Weston, Kull and Ramsey had originally formed a band called Narcissus in 1985 and were performing cover tunes from prog bands such as Yes and Genesis. They played their first gigs as Echolyn in clubs around Philadelphia throughout 1990. At the same time, they were writing original material, some of which would end up on their first self-titled ECHOLYN CD released in 1991. The night the CD was released they opened for Allan Holdsworth.

Some have said it was the addition of classically trained keyboardist Buzby that took the group to it's full potential. Be that as it may, there was no question that, with a CD out, the band began to pick up momentum and were soon playing the larger clubs and selling out virtually every time. They started distributing their CD overseas and continued writing new material.

Their second CD, SUFFOCATING THE BLOOM, was another step forward, with the showcase twenty eight minute track *A Suite for the Every Man* displaying a maturing writing and arranging style. They quickly followed that up in 1993 with the all acoustic . . . AND EVERY BLOSSOM, which turned out to be their last independent release. In August 1993 the band was signed to Epic Records, a division of Sony Music. This was greeted by a collective gasp throughout the prog underground. One of their own was signed to a major label, could this mean that prog was about to shed it's underground status and hit the mainstream? Or would it mean that Echolyn would be forced to streamline their sound to accommodate the less adventurous ears of a mainstream label? In the end, neither one happened.

The band spent most of October and November 1994 on the road. They had completed recording AS THE WORLD and were performing much of the material live. Taking a break over Christmas they planned to return to touring in March of 1995 in preparation for the CD's release. The tour took them into Canada and then to ProgDay '95, a prog festival in North Carolina. The 1995 Sony release of AS THE WORLD showed Echolyn creating and performing music every bit as challenging as their independent releases. In fact, many would say it was their best material, aided by three months in the best studio yet afforded them, with corresponding equipment and production. AS THE WORLD was very much a progressive rock album, with the songs divided into three movements, a beginning, a middle and an end. While many of the songs are in the 4 to 5 minute range, they're joined together to create a seamless composition. It's hard to know when one ends and another starts. Compositionally, you're greeted with a

dynamic intensity one moment which gives way to pastoral relaxation the next. It's very much a prog trait to write about philosophical, even metaphysical issues and, in this regard, Echolyn have, more than many bands, set the standard. The group was not afraid to tackle the issues of human frailty, life and death, and the hereafter, as well as values such as honesty and integrity — not easy things to write about. Their first album contained inspiration from Ayn Rand, while AS THE WORLD borrowed from CS Lewis. The major label CD was greeted with glowing reviews from virtually every prog publication and a collective sigh that Echolyn just might have beaten the system.

One week after their performance at ProgDay '95, seemingly at the height of the band's rise to popularity, Tom Hyatt announced that he was leaving. His departure turned out to be one of the determining factors leading to the dissolution of Echolyn. Not able to find a suitable or compatible replacement, Chris Buzby left to form his own group Finneus Gauge and released the more jazz oriented MORE ONCE MORE in 1997. The remaining members of Echolyn carried on as Still, releasing one CD entitled ALMOST ALWAYS, and then changed their name again to Almost Always and released another CD called GOD POUNDS HIS NAILS. Both these releases focused more on a "grunge" guitar sound and less on the keyboard sound of Echolyn.

Echolyn had one last gasp with the CD WHEN THE SWEET TURNS SOUR which contains a number of demo tracks and other material that was originally destined for a second Sony CD. While Finneus Gauge and Almost Always continue in their own musical directions, guitarist and vocalist Brett Kull has said that Echolyn would resurface in some form in the future.

- o ECHOLYN (1991 Independent)
- o SUFFOCATING THE BLOOM (1992 Independent)
- o ...And Every Blossom (1993 Independent)
- o AS THE WORLD (1995 Epic Records)
- o WHEN THE SWEET TURNS SOUR (1996 Syn-Phonic)

# ~ 12 ~
# Eloy (Germany)

In his book *The Time Machine*, H.G. Wells writes about the human race starting over. The name he gives to the people making the new start is Eloy. Seeing the parallel about starting over and the emerging music scene in Germany in the late 60's, Frank Bornemann chose the name Eloy to aptly describe his band which would break out of the "cover band" mentality that was so prevalent at the time. Thirty years and countless recordings later the Eloy continue to break new ground.

Eloy came together in 1969 and, like so many other bands of the day, got their start playing cover tunes before venturing into the studio, in Hamburg in 1971, to record their first self-titled LP. Initially, the band consisted of three composers and finding a musical direction proved difficult. After the departure of vocalist / guitarist Erich Schriever, Bornemann assumed the guitars and the leadership role. Also in the band were Manfred Wieczorke (keyboards) and Fritz Ranbow (drums.) Under Bornemann's leadership, the Eloy went headlong in the progressive rock direction and were signed to EMI's Electrola label releasing INSIDE in 1973, followed the next year by FLOATING. It was during these years they undertook their first tours of England, playing support for other early prog bands Beggars Opera and East of Eden. The next big step for Eloy came with the recording of POWER AND PASSION in 1975. The album sold well, but, because of internal dissension over musical direction, the band broke up. Keyboardist Wieczorke landed in Jane and Bornemann put together a new Eloy with individuals who more fully shared his musical vision of concept albums with symphonic arrangements. This led to the highly creative period which saw the release of DAWN, OCEAN and SILENT CRIES AND MIGHTY ECHOES, all classics of the state of the ary of progressive rock during the mid-70's. The band was made up of Bornemann (guitars), Klaus Peter Matziol (bass), Detlev Schmidtchen (keyboards) and Jurgen Rosenthal (drums) and it was with this lineup that Eloy became one of the biggest groups in Germany at the time. When it came to recording, they were calling the shots. If an orchestra was required, they got it; more time in the studio, they got it.

But all good things must come to an end, and so it was with this version of Eloy when both Schmidtchen and Rosenthal chose to pursue solo careers. Replacements were brought in for the 1980 LP COLOURS and the next few years were ones of turmoil for Eloy as members struggled yet again over musical direction, with some pushing for a hard rock sound while Bornemann was still insisting on the progressive rock vein. Over this period Eloy released PLANETS, TIME TO TURN (part 2 of Planets), PERFORMANCE and finally, in 1984, METROMANIA, after which thay all went their own separate ways. For the next couple years Bornemann got involved with producing. In 1988 he met up with Michael Gerlach and the two decided that, with the advancement of musical technology, they were now able to create the music of Eloy as a duo. The result of this partnership was 1988's RA and 1992's DESTINATION, both of which did quite well on the charts so long after Eloy's prime years. With interest running high, many of the original members assembled in the studio to create new or updated versions of some of their classic tracks for the two volume set CHRONICLES released in the mid-90's. As a testament to the enduring strength of the Eloy, their first official fan club was created in 1995. Throughout much of the year the band toured to celebrate their 25th Anniversary. All performances were sold out. The band released THE TIDES RETURN FOREVER which is very much in the classic Eloy style and followed that release in 1998 with OCEANS II, a sequel, of sorts, to their top selling album of 1977. This release showed Eloy at the top of their form, writing in the classic style but recording with the aid of modern sound and technology.

The current lineup of the Eloy on the road is Bornemann (guitars), Michael Gerlach (keyboards), Klaus Peter Matziol (bass), Steve Mann (guitars, keyboards), Bodo Schopf (drums) and Bettina Lux and Susanne Schatzle on backing vocals. When not on the road or in the studio, Eloy's main man, Frank Bornemann, spends his days as a producer working with many young bands looking for their first big break.

- o ELOY (1971 Philips)
- o INSIDE (1973 EMI Electrola)
- o FLOATING (1974 EMI Electrola)
- o POWER AND THE PASSION (1975 EMI Electrola)
- o DAWN (1976 EMI Electrola)
- o OCEAN (1977 EMI Electrola)
- o LIVE (1978 EMI Electrola)
- o SILENT CRIES AND MIGHTY ECHOES (1979 EMI Electrola)

- COLOURS (1980 EMI Electrola)
- PLANETS (1981 EMI Electrola)
- TIME AND TURN (1982 EMI Electrola)
- PERFORMANCE (1983 EMI Electrola)
- METROMANIA (1984 EMI Electrola)
- CODE NAME WILDGEESE [Soundtrack] (1985 SW Milan)
- RA (1988 Revolver)
- RARITIES (1991 EMI Electrola)
- DESTINATION (1992 SPV)
- CHRONICLES I (1993 SPV)
- CHRONICLES II (1994 SPV)
- THE TIDES RETURN FOREVER (1994 SPV)
- THE BEST OF ELOY VOL. II (1996 EMI Electrola)
- OCEAN II — THE ANSWER (1998 BMG Gun)

# ~ 13 ~
# Emerson, Lake & Palmer (England)

One of the first progressive rock supergroups, ELP evolved from three high profile bands of the late 60's, namely The Nice, Atomic Rooster and King Crimson. In late 1969 King Crimson was supporting The Nice on an American tour. Keith Emerson and Greg Lake discovered that they shared a musical vision, so when The Nice broke up in March of 1970, Emerson, who'd already established himself as a showman with his keyboard antics, renewed acquaintances with Lake and they started looking for a drummer. They eventually chose Atomic Rooster's Carl Palmer. ELP were very much a band to see live, although their recordings were nothing short of progressive rock spectaculars.

Emerson Lake & Palmer played their first "unofficial" gig on August 23rd at the Guild Hall in Plymouth, but it was their second appearance, before 600,000 music lovers at the Isle of Wight festival August 29th 1970, that generated the exposure they wanted. They performed *Pictures at an Exhibition* on a bill that included The Moody Blues, The Who, Jethro Tull, Jimi Hendrix and many others.

The pre-release publicity for their first recording was in high gear and expectations were high as to what this new breed of progressive rock band might accomplish in the studio. ELP didn't disappoint. A mixture of instrumental and vocal tracks with a trace of pop, mixed with large doses of adventurous

musical virtuosity, gentle piano and acoustic guitar trading licks, mixed at times with sonic explosions from Carl Palmer. Their first self-titled release was an overnight success in both the United States and Britain. It even produced the hugely successful single *Lucky Man.* Their next two releases, TARKUS and PICTURES AT AN EXHIBITION, followed in the same successful manner. In 1972 ELP released TRILOGY reflecting a more mature band compositionally and the tour which followed featured all the latest staging machinery including an elevating and

*Emerson, Lake & Palmer*

rotating piano.

In an effort to maintain as much creative control as possible, ELP created their own record label called Manticore. This label became home to not only ELP's work, but also other prog bands such as Italians PFM and Banco. Their first Manticore release was BRAIN SALAD SURGERY, a classically prog-themed effort pitting man against a harsh technological world. The years 1975 and 1976 were quiet ones for ELP, although behind the scenes they were working on solo and band projects that would ultimately surface in their next releases in 1977 as the double LP WORKS VOLUME 1 and the solo efforts of WORKS VOLUME 2.

ELP's next recording, LOVE BEACH, was a contractual recording for Atlantic and is perhaps their most controversial. It's constantly panned by fans and critics alike and yet contains all the hallmarks of an ELP release including a classical reworking and, most notably, the twenty minute epic *Memoirs of an Officer and a Gentleman*. It's become a cliché to say that ELP were just going through the motions in this recording. But, in fact, the music holds up quite well in the ELP catalogue. One thing was for sure, the band had grown tired of the direction they'd been going in, so ELP officially announced their breakup at a media conference in December of 1979. Carl Palmer formed PM then got involved with Asia, Emerson focused on movie soundtracks, and Lake concentrated on solo recordings.

When they came together eight years later, it was a somewhat different ELP that appeared. Carl Palmer, still busy with commitments to Asia, was not available, but Emerson and Lake were ready. In a not so subtle publicity move they recruited noted session drummer Cozy Powell to be the "P" for their next release, 1986's EMERSON LAKE AND POWELL, providing fans with some of their best work to date. This union was not to last and Palmer returned in 1992 for the ELP release BLACK MOON. This was a very 90's ELP, with a set of radio ready songs, and stripped down and recorded almost live-to-tape in an attempt to capture the band's live energy. While many were happy to see ELP back, others were hoping for a return to slightly more adventurous compositions. Both groups were disappointed with the band's next release, IN THE HOT SEAT. It even disappointed the band. While many of the traditional ELP elements are there, they're produced in such a streamlined or mainstream manner that they lose all sense of uniqueness, sounding instead simple, plain and ordinary. The group spent much of 1997 as the opening act for Jethro Tull, performing an abbreviated one hour set of their most popular songs. ELP returned to the studio in 1998 to begin work on new material. Before long however, the internet was ablaze with the news that Greg Lake had decided to leave the band over musical differences and production credits. ELP's future seemed in doubt, like it had so many times over the previous 30 years. From the very beginning of their career ELP established themselves as a temperamental, technically skilled band that was not afraid to tour. Their recordings showcase their highly developed musical skills combined with more than average showmanship, a balance of harmony and dissonance, acoustics and electronics.

o EMERSON LAKE & PALMER (1970 Cotillion)
o TARKUS (1971 Cotillion)
o PICTURES AT AN EXHIBITION (1971 Cotillion)
o TRILOGY (1972 Cotillion)
o BRAIN SALAD SURGERY (1973 Manticore)
o WELCOME BACK MY FRIENDS (1974 Manticore)
o WORKS (1977 Atlantic)
o WORKS VOL. 2 (1977 Atlantic)
o LOVE BEACH (1978 Atlantic)
o IN CONCERT (1979 Atlantic)
o THE BEST OF ELP (1980 Atlantic)
o EMERSON LAKE & POWELL (1986 Polygram)
o BLACK MOON (1992 Victory)
o THE ATLANTIC YEARS (1992 Atlantic)
o LIVE AT THE ROYAL ALBERT HALL (1993 Victory)
o RETURN OF THE MANITCORE [Box Set] (1993 Victory)
o IN THE HOT SEAT (1994 Victory)
o WORKS LIVE (1996 Rhino)
o LIVE AT THE ISLE OF WIGHT 1970 (1997 Manticore)
o ELP IN CONCERT ON THE KING BISCUIT FLOWER HOUR (1997 KBFH Records)
o THEN AND NOW (1998 Eagle)

# ~ 14 ~
# The Enid (England)

The music of The Enid is perhaps the ultimate blending of orchestral arrangements in a rock setting. The instrumentation is typically rock — guitars, drums and keyboards — but, for most of their material, that's where the comparison ends. The music created is majestic, panoramic, dynamic and definitely not rock. If anything, The Enid is Robert John Godfrey, and although he has been ably assisted over the years by a series of highly skilled musicians, most notably and lengthily by Steven Stewart, the core of the band rests with Godfrey.

In 1969 through to 1971 Godfrey was working with Barclay James Harvest. His

role was that of arranger and conductor of the small orchestra that they were incorporating into their early classics. In 1972 Godfrey became acquainted with Tony Stratton Smith and was signed to Smith's Charisma label. Later that year he wrote and recorded a solo LP entitled THE FALL OF HYPERION. For the lyrics Godfrey relied on the inspiration of Keats, and the music was already foreshadowing the orchestral Enid style, although, at the time, he relied more on piano and Mellotron than synths.

The Enid were formed in June 1974 by the meeting of Godfrey (keyboards), Stephen Stewart (guitar) and Francis Lickerish (guitar.) January 1976 saw the release of their first LP, IN THE REGION OF SUMMER STARS. The band was fleshed out with the addition of Dave Story (drums), Glen Tollet (keyboards), and Neil Kavanaugh (bass.) They were quickly signed to a worldwide deal with EMI International as the distributor and all seemed rosy. A major label with worldwide distribution was nothing to be sneezed at. Shortly after this auspicious event, touring began, as did personnel changes with Terry Pack (bass) and Charlie Elston (keyboards) brought in to replace Kavanaugh and Tollet. The next release, AERIE FAERIE NONSENSE in 1977, came at the height of the punk music phenomenon, and while many progressive rock bands suffered at the media onslaught, The Enid, in their own way, managed to garner media attention. A change in labels resulted in two more releases: SIX PIECES (1978) and TOUCH ME (1979.) Unfortunately, Pye records was very unsure of what to make of the band and as a result promotion suffered. Making his debut at this time was Willie Gilmore (keyboards) and shortly after that Robbie Dobson (percussion.) During these years the Enid's musical style continued to evolve displaying fewer rock influences and incorporating more and more traditionally classical elements and motifs. Technology had allowed the complete masking of traditionally rock instruments and Godfrey's compositional abilities had turned them into extensions of a classical orchestra. The instrumental music displayed all the grandeur of a classical symphony and none of the rock and roll blues associated with guitar, bass, drums and keyboards.

In 1980 they parted company with Pye and then, in 1981, a lengthy tour set Godfrey and Lickerish at odds with each other and Lickerish left — taking with him Willie Gillmore, followed in succession by Martin Russell, and then Chris North. It was down to Godfrey and Stewart. Together they forged ahead. 1983's SOMETHING WICKED THIS WAY COMES saw The Enid emerge after a couple of tumultuous years filled with illness and with legal wrangling with EMI Records. It also marked the appearance of vocals for the first time. Thematically the album focused on the threat of nuclear war and the planet's impending doom. They were joined by former member Chris North on a session basis. The technology being what it was, the Enid were able to create the sound that they wanted even as a trio. Back in the studio they released the double LP THE SPELL in 1984 and then SALOME in 1986. But all good things come to an end and that last release displayed a growing divergence of musical direction between Godfrey and Stewart. Over the past few years Stewart had wanted to move in a more commercial direction but was restrained to a large degree by Godfrey's overriding vision of what The Enid was all about. They recorded THE SEED AND THE SOWER in 1988 knowing it would be their final collaborative effort. Nothing more was heard from The Enid until the 1994 release of TRIPPING THE LIGHT FANTASTIC. Godfrey teamed up with a group of younger musicians, once again with the idea of furthering his lofty musical goals. TRIPPING . . . shows The Enid incorporating their early classical structure and blending it together with a very contemporary musical direction. It's nowhere near pop, but some of the compositions actually develop a groove. It's upbeat, even with a sense of urgency. The band continued to develop this new direction, as well as the traditional Enid style, with SUNDIALER in 1995 and the critically well received WHITE GODDESS in 1998.

More than anything The Enid continue to be a powerful influence in the prog world with their do-or-die attitude, as well as their desire to do it all themselves but do it right. This attitude holds true for everything from their composing to their recording and distribution. Their successful battle with EMI records to win back the rights to their early recordings is an inspiration for all up-and-coming bands — they strove for their musical goals and weren't distracted by searching for the big record deal.

- o IN THE REGION OF SUMMER STARS (1976 Enid)
- o AERIE FAERIE NONSENSE (1977 Enid)
- o TOUCH ME (1979 Enid)
- o SIX PIECES (1979 Enid)
- o LIVE AT THE HAMMERSMITH (1983 Enid)
- o SOMETHING WICKED THIS WAY COMES (1983 Enid)
- o THE SPELL (1984 Enid)
- o LOVERS AND FOOLS (1986 Enid)
- o SALOME (1986 Enid)
- o THE SEED AND THE SOWER (1988 Enid)
- o THE FINAL NOISE (1988 Enid)
- o TRIPPING THE LIGHT FANTASTIC (1994 Enid)
- o SUNDIALER (1995 Enid)
- o WHITE GODDESS (1998 Enid)

# ~ **15** ~

# The Flower Kings (Sweden)

When it comes to the symphonic progressive rock of the 90's, one of the all time favourites has turned out to be Sweden's The Flower Kings. Like many a prog band before them, they boast influences which include bands such as Yes and Gentle Giant, as well as a host of other musical genres including classical, opera and jazz. The music, whether it's a one minute piece or a twenty five minute epic, is dynamic and dramatic, containing many moods and much musical virtuosity. The Flower Kings are influential for being one of the large group of Swedish bands to propel prog well into the 90's by keeping it sounding fresh and alive.

The roots of The Flower Kings and Roine Stolt go back to the Swedish band Kaipa where Stolt was guitarist. Kaipa produced three LP's of vintage although not earth shattering progressive rock in the mid-to-late 70's. Kaipa were often compared to Camel in that they were able to craft music that was complex and yet thoroughly memorable with strong melodies. Much like his later work, Stolt's guitar is featured throughout but doesn't dominate the material. After Kaipa's demise, Stolt spent time as a solo artist, producer and session player on the Swedish music scene. During his solo career he produced three LP's: FANTASIA (1979), the more pop oriented BEHIND THE WALLS (1985) and THE LONELY HEARTBEAT (1989.)

In late 1993 Stolt got together with drummer Jamie Salazar and percussionist Hasse Bruniusson to record THE FLOWER KING, an album that took him back to his progressive roots. Following its release, he put a band together to rekindle the creative interplay that he missed working as a solo artist. Both Salazar and Bruniusson agreed to join the new group. They were quickly joined by Stolt's brother Michael (bass) and long time friend Tomas Bodin (keyboards.) The group was asked to perform at a local prog-rock festival in Sweden and, with only four hours of rehearsal, the band worked well together on stage and the audience loved it. Thus The Flower Kings as a group was born.

The Flower Kings signature sound is based on both Stolt's guitar playing and Bodin's keyboard work. Stolt's technical style has often been compared to other guitarists such as Alan Holdsworth, Andy Latimer and Jeff Beck. On the other side of the stage, classically trained Bodin's keyboard lineup of Hammond organ, Mellotron and various analog synthesizers leaves no doubt about the genre of music, its pure progressive rock.

With the success of the first recording the band returned to the studio and produced two excellent examples of symphonic prog — BACK IN THE WORLD OF ADVENTURES (1995) and RETROPOLIS (1996) — each receiving more accolades than the previous. The band was on a roll, and judging by the speed with which they were putting out albums, they were on a mission. In between recording sessions the band kept up a very solid touring schedule through much of Europe. The double CD release STARDUST WE ARE in 1997 established The Flower Kings as one of the leading symphonic prog bands of the 90's and featured almost two hours of the highest quality material including the twenty five minute closing title track. The release turned out to be the band's biggest seller yet and won them praise around the world. Critics were hailing the CD as awesome, and throwing around terms such as masterpiece.

The Flower Kings played a series of successful North American gigs including Progfest '97 in Los Angeles and then, later in the year, performed throughout Europe, Brazil and Canada.

Having recorded five albums since 1994, two of which were double CDs, The Flower Kings rank as one of the most prolific bands around today. Even in the midst of all the recording and touring, Stolt still found time to record a solo CD in 1997 entitled HYDROPHONIA, while Bodin released his solo entitled AN ORDINARY NIGHT IN MY ORDINARY LIFE in 1996. Having barely finished promoting the solo CD, the Flower Kings were back in the studio laying down tracks for their next recording. So full of musical ideas, The Flower Kings' next recording turned out to be another double CD entitled appropriately FLOWERPOWER. Released in January of 1999, it featured the epic composition *Garden of Dreams* clocking in at sixty minutes.

Like many of the prog bands of the 70's, The Flower Kings' music is based on strong melodies with intricate arrangements taking a bit of a back seat. Even so, the music is still very dramatic and full of twists and turns. With Stolt solidly heading up The Flower Kings and his compositions sonically shaped by the other band members, the group looks set to tackle the new millennium. The future of progressive rock looks very bright indeed.

- ROINE STOLT / THE FLOWER KING (1994 Foxtrot)
- BACK IN THE WORLD OF ADVENTURES (1995 Foxtrot)
- RETROPOLIS (1996 Foxtrot)
- STARDUST WE ARE (1997 Foxtrot)
- FLOWERPOWER (1999 Foxtrot)

# ~ 16 ~
# Focus (Holland)

Focus was one of the pioneering progressive rock bands from Europe. They became a major concert attraction throughout the Continent playing extended songs with lots of classical motifs thrown in. They produced a uniquely instrumental progressive rock with traditional folk and jazz influences. Their music revolved around the heady interplay of flute and guitar while vocals were kept to a minimum.

Formed in Amsterdam in 1969 with the meeting of Jan Akkerman (guitar), Martin Dresden (bass), Hans Cleuver (drums) and Thijs Van Leer (keyboards, flute), they produced their first recording, IN AND OUT OF FOCUS, in early 1971. This first recorded effort shows the band's blend of folk, classical and jazz into a rock format already well integrated. Their second album, MOVING WAVES, came out later that same year containing the six minute *Hocus Pocus* and the twenty three minute epic *Eruption*. While the band was working on their third LP late in 1971, they remixed a shorter version of *Hocus Pocus* and released it to radio. It wound up a Top 10 Hit. Its quirky and unique blend of rocking instrumental with delicate flute flourishes, highlighted by an over the top yodel, caught the ears of influential radio programmers in Europe and the United States. The single became a smash

hit for the band, and suddenly they were in the spotlight. During the creation of their third LP Cleuver and Dresden left the band and were replaced by Pierre Van Der Linden (drums) and Bert Ruiter (bass.) This new lineup produced the double LP FOCUS 3 in 1972.

They undertook three short, but very successful, British concert tours which earned them Melody Maker's "Brightest Hope for 1972" and The New Musical Express "Best New Talent of 1972" awards. FOCUS AT THE RAINBOW — a live album recorded in London during the British tour — was released in 1973.

If you thought they were out of ideas, you were wrong because 1974's HAMBURGER CONCERTO showed them at their peak with the side-long title track. This was followed by SHIP OF MEMORIES, essentially left over material from the previous albums sessions. The always tempestuous relationship between Akkerman and Van Leer came to a head around this time with Akkerman bowing out of the band. New guitarist Phillip Catherine took the band in a more vocal direction with the 1978 release FOCUS CON PROBY. This proved to be the last official Focus release for some time. Although band members continued to work on a variety of solo projects, nothing was heard from them together until FOCUS-AKKERMAN & LEER released in 1985. The LP's contents clearly demonstrated that the magic hadn't left, with the compositions still displaying their unique blend of rock and classical elements. It was not to last however, and following this release the two again went their separate ways. Time passed and it wasn't until 1996 that Van Leer decided to reunite with bassist Bert Ruiter for a series of live performances that took them across the United States and points in Canada, which took them into 1997. The band this time around consisted of not only Van Leer and Ruiter, but also Hans Gleuver, Mark Deron and Menno Grootves.

Over the years the music of Focus matured and some say peaked with HAMBURGER CONCERTO containing the smoothest blend of rock, classical and jazz with a strong European influence. Whether this latest version of Focus adds anything new to the musical catalogue remains to be seen. But for prog fans interested in some great guitar, keyboard and flute work they need look no further than Focus.

o IN AND OUT OF FOCUS (1971 Sire)
o MOVING WAVES (1971 Sire)
o FOCUS III (1972 Sire)
o AT THE RAINBOW (1973 Sire)
o HAMBURGER CONCERTO (1974 Atco)
o MOTHER FOCUS (1975 Atco)
o SHIP OF MEMORIES (1976 Sire)
o DUTCH MASTERS (1976 Compilation)
o FOCUS CON PROBY (1978 Harvest)
o FOCUS - AKKERMAN & LEER (1985 Vertigo)

# ~ 17 ~
# Gabriel, Peter (England)

To progressive rock fans Peter Gabriel will always be known as the former lead singer of Genesis. The fact that he chose to leave the band during the height of their early days to pursue a solo career only contributes to the legend. It was during the creation of THE LAMB LIES DOWN ON BROADWAY that the pressures and demands from both Genesis and Gabriel's family caused him to rethink his future. While on tour he let the band know that he was going to leave.

Gabriel's solo career incorporates many diverse world and ethnic influences into his uniquely styled progressive material. His first album appeared in 1977 and, with the help of producer Bob Ezrin, managed not to sound much like Genesis at all other than for a track like *Moribund the Burgermeister*. The album also contained *Solsbury Hill* which received some radio airplay and spoke of his departure from Genesis. The album featured a stripped-down sound and seemed to capture the mood of the moment. It received good reviews all around, as did the tour undertaken to support it. Gabriel created a loose-knit group of musicians that you could loosely call a band, but also began working with a variety of noted solo artists. Each release took on it's own sound depending on the specific influences Gabriel choose to incorporate.

Gabriel had decided not to bother naming each album, instead choosing to handle it numerically, hence PETER GABRIEL II was released in 1978 and this time was produced by Robert Fripp of King Crimson fame. Fripp also performed on the album providing a little more experimental and dissonant framework for this second release. It was PETER GABRIEL III that pushed him over the top in terms of coming out from under the shadow of Genesis. Here, under the guidance of hot producer-of-the-day Steve Lillywhite, he achieved a radio hit with *Games Without Frontiers*, and a fair amount of notoriety with the song *Biko*, written about the South African poet and political activist Steven Biko. For this release Gabriel had settled on rhythm being the driving force for his compositions. The subtle textures were still there, but more as frilly attachments to the groove. Ultimately pressure from the record company's marketing department provoked Gabriel to title his fourth release SECURITY, however the title on the vinyl release only appears on the record itself and not on the outside sleeve. Produced by Gabriel and David Lord, we begin to see the incorporation of the world beat into Gabriel's compositional style. Lyrically he continued focusing on human rights-based issues and the album produced the hit single *Shock the Monkey*.

As a true artist, Gabriel's dabbling in the world of music videos allowed him to present his music to a wider audience. His early work here helped put him at the forefront of music and evolving technology. Yet another artistic side of Gabriel came with the establishment of an organization to promote world music called WOMAD. For the first WOMAD Festival, in 1982, Gabriel handed over chores to others and things went undone. The organization was about to collapse, the festival was a financial disaster and he was on the hook financially. Coming to his aid, Genesis offered to perform a re-union gig with all profits going to help repay WOMAD's debts. The gig took place in 1984 at Milton Keynes, and while it poured rain most of the evening, was well attended and fans went home overjoyed at seeing the original band back together, even if it was for just one evening.

In 1983, PLAYS LIVE was released, followed in 1985 with a soundtrack for the film BIRDY. Having done a full album incorporating little more than rhythm and textures, Gabriel chose to go in a very different direction. It had been four years since his last studio album, but in 1986 he created SO, this time with the album title printed on the back of the sleeve. Here the biggest influences were R&B, Funk and, of course, worldbeat. It was his most accessible release yet, produced

by Daniel Lanois of U2 fame. This album helped make Gabriel a world-wide celebrity thanks to the huge hits *Big Time* and *Sledgehammer*. Knowning him as a perfectionist who took his time, the record company decided that a greatest hits package was in order and, in 1990, put together SHAKING THE TREE: SIXTEEN GOLDEN GREATS. As the title states, it was not so much a hits package as it was a "best of" collection.

In 1992 Gabriel released US his first studio album since 1986. It was a more introspective set of songs dealing with the painful side of human relationships. This was the material on which his hugely successful Secret World Tour was based. Always the showman, Gabriel shines live, and listening to the live recording one misses a good portion of the experience. Nonetheless, a live double album, SECRET WORLD LIVE, was released in 1994. Since then reports continue to surface of his efforts in the studio. For Gabriel recording is a painful process of creating perfection.

- ○ PETER GABRIEL I (1977 Atco)
- ○ PETER GABRIEL II (1978 Atco)
- ○ PETER GABRIEL III (1980 Geffen)
- ○ PETER GABRIEL IV [Security] (1982 Geffen)
- ○ PLAYS LIVE (1983 Geffen)
- ○ MUSIC FROM THE FILM "BIRDY" (1985 Geffen)
- ○ SO (1986 Geffen)
- ○ PASSION [SOUNDTRACK] (1989 Geffen)
- ○ SHAKING THE TREE: SIXTEEN GOLDEN GREATS (1990 Geffen)
- ○ US (1992 Geffen)
- ○ REVISITED (1992 Atlantic)
- ○ SECRET WORLD LIVE (1994 Geffen)

# ~ 18 ~
# Genesis (England)

When it comes to the progressive rock genre Genesis can proudly claim a position with what's come to be known as the "big six". The symphonic prog style that Genesis developed had a tremendous influence on future progressive rock musicians around the world. Their music had all of the elements of drama, intensity, warmth, intricate chord changes, a blend of electric and acoustic dynamics, and, of course, philosophical lyrics.

Formed by core members Peter Gabriel (vocals), Mike Rutherford (bass), Tony Banks (keyboards), Anthony Phillips (guitar) and John Silver (drums), their first pop oriented release, FROM GENESIS TO REVELATION, produced, by pop entrepreneur Jonathan King, went virtually nowhere in late 1969. As a result of the negative reaction to the band, Silver was replaced with John Mayhew and whenever Peter Gabriel wasn't trying to line up gigs for them, they rehearsed for hours on end. Out of this dedication to perfection came their first progressive rock LP, TRESPASS, with their trademark set-closer *The Knife*. It was October of 1970. The band had been performing as much as possible, so that each of the songs on the recording had been worked through in a live setting. By the end of

copyright 1984 Phil Anderson / KAOS2000 Magazine

its first year of release TRESPASS had sold approximately 6,000 copies world wide — a vast improvement over the paltry 600-700 sales of their first LP.

The pressures of recording and touring began to take their toll and original members Phillips and Mayhew left to be replaced by Steve Hackett and Phil Collins. It was this lineup that created NURSERY CRYME in 1971, a major step forward for the band. All of the growing musical maturity was fronted by an ever more flamboyant Peter Gabriel who's bizarre costumes and song introductions only fueled the band's stage persona. At the time, Genesis was still not that well known outside of London, yet they found themselves on the record charts in Italy when NURSERY CRYME reached the No. 4 spot. Young Italians had never really taken to standard rock and roll. Having grown up in a tradition rich with classical and operatic music. English progressive rock was just right for their ears. Genesis was hugely responsible for influencing the budding Italian progressive rock scene. The band recorded FOXTROT in 1972 with the epic masterpiece *Supper's Ready*, followed by SELLING ENGLAND BY THE POUND in 1973 and a minor chart

copyright 1984 Phil Anderson / KAOS2000 Magazine

appearance with *I Know What I Like*, and then the ambitious double record set THE LAMB LIES DOWN ON BROADWAY in 1974.

It was at this point that Gabriel announced that he didn't want to become a rock star and chose to leave. Many critics announced the death of Genesis, but the band had other ideas. They went into the studio to start on their new release and look for a new vocalist. After many auditions it was that decided Phil Collins would step into the front spotlight and 1976's A TRICK OF THE TAIL showed an invigorated Genesis, slightly more aggressive, but every bit as prog. They followed that release with the more melodic and even more dramatic WIND & WUTHERING in early 1977. It was while recording WIND & WUTHERING that Steve Hackett decided that he needed more creative space and left to concentrate on his budding solo career. 1978's tongue in cheek AND THEN THERE WERE THREE showed the band in a state of transition as they began writing shorter, less complicated material and achieving their first significant pop success with *Follow You Follow Me*. Their last overtly prog release was DUKE, with it's semi-conceptual nature and more adventurous compositions. Still Collins' influence was becoming stronger and the hit *Misunderstanding* came mostly from his pen. With 1981's ABACAB came a new approach to writing. The band members, all working on solo projects by this time, would assemble in their studio and begin jamming. Out of this jamming the "best" material was developed and recorded. This approach was employed throughout the releases of GENESIS in 1983, INVISIBLE TOUCH in 1986 and WE CAN'T DANCE in 1991.

When it came to mass appeal and commercial hit records, the band was flying. Genesis ruled the airwaves and concert tours during the 80's and early 90's. Then, in 1996, Phil Collins announced that he was leaving. Banks and Rutherford, determined to carry on, recruited the virtually unknown vocalist Ray Wilson and released CALLING ALL STATIONS in 1997. It was time for a change. The sound was darker, aggressive and moody — not quite a return to the early days, but quite a departure from their bright, upbeat 80's sound. However, it was a tough act to follow and the band faltered. The CD failed to satisfy both the fans from the 80's and those from the earlier days. A world tour didn't sell well and the American portion was canceled when Genesis took time to refocus.

Genesis helped create the progressive rock genre. They carved out a sound that stands as a benchmark to this day. They pioneered progressive rock at a time when the instruments themselves were going through development from Mellotrons to simple synthesizers to digital samplers. The music was always textured and exquisitely crafted. Always a good place to start.

- FROM GENESIS TO REVELATION (1969 DCC)
- TRESPASS (1970 MCA)
- NURSERY CRYME (1971 Atlantic)
- FOXTROT (1972 Atlantic)
- SELLING ENGLAND BY THE POUND (1973 Atlantic)
- GENESIS LIVE (1973 Atlantic)
- THE LAMB LIES DOWN ON BROADWAY (1974 Atlantic)
- A TRICK OF THE TAIL (1976 Atlantic)
- WIND & WUTHERING (1977 Atlantic)
- SPOT THE PIGEON EP (1977 Atlantic)
- SECONDS OUT (1977 Atlantic)
- AND THEN THERE WERE THREE (1978 Atlantic)
- DUKE (1980 Atlantic)
- ABACAB (1981 Atlantic)
- THREE SIDES LIVE (1982 Atlantic)
- GENESIS (1983 Atlantic)
- INVISIBLE TOUCH (1986 Atlantic)
- WE CAN'T DANCE (1991 Atlantic)
- THE WAY WE WALK: THE SHORTS (1992 Atlantic)
- THE WAY WE WALK: THE LONGS (1993 Atlantic)
- CALLING ALL STATIONS (1997 Atlantic)

# ~ 19 ~

# Gentle Giant (England)

Gentle Giant was one of the first bands to successfully merge medieval madrigals with snippets of classics into what was some of the most original progressive rock. They created a style of traditional sounding early English folk music that seemed to hop around from verse to chorus. Given their use of non-traditional instruments and their adventurous multi-part harmonies, Gentle Giant have been labeled one of the most complex groups of any age.

In late 1969, brothers Derek and Ray Shulman decided to put together a more adventurous outfit. Based in Portsmouth, they had gone through the late 60's known as Simon Dupree and The Big Sound. They even had a hit single called *Kites*. However, the fact that none of them was actually named Simon Dupree, and a growing dissatisfaction with playing music that they weren't very keen on, caused the group to split. By 1970 they'd joined forces with blues guitarist Gary Green and keyboardist Kerry Minnear, who came to the band with a Royal Academy degree in composition. Together they formed Gentle Giant. They'd heard King Crimson and Yes and were fascinated by that whole sound. Their first LP, GENTLE GIANT, was released in late 1970, but didn't receive much attention. Their second release, ACQUIRING THE TASTE, saw them solidify their unique sound and start to get noticed.

By the time of their third and fourth releases, THREE FRIENDS and OCTOPUS respectively, they began to gather a small but dedicated following in North America, particularly in the French speaking Canadian province of Quebec. The band eventually toured there and left the seeds of inspiration that stand to this day. Quebec has always had more than the average number of prog bands, and in many cases they've displayed a style influenced to varying degrees by Gentle Giant.

In late 1973 they released IN A GLASS HOUSE. Internally the pressure was building and Phil Shulman departed. Even the group admitted they were not particularly happy with how the album turned out, yet it remains a favourite of fans. In true prog fashion, Gentle Giant's next release, THE POWER AND THE GLORY in 1974, was a concept album, influenced in part by the Watergate scandal that was in the news during this time. Perhaps due in part to the extra publicity, sales for the album in the U.S. were strong. As a result of those strong sales, their 1975 release, FREE HAND, also did well and did much to build on their America following. Strangely, they were bigger in America than in England during this time. FREE HAND, while still displaying the bands' penchant for complicated compositions, also tends to "rock out" more than their previous releases, an element that was not lost on their growing American fan base. A change in drummers brought in John Weathers for the next release, INTERVIEW in 1976, and a live double album followed. The lineup of Derek and Ray Shulman, Gary Green, Kerry Minnear and John Weathers released two further albums in the late 70's: THE MISSING PIECE and GIANT FOR A DAY.

By 1980, it seemed the band was desperate for a major breakthrough. So much so that they enlisted the help of noted radio programmer Lee Abrams to help with their next release. Abrams had been responsible for creating the successful AOR — or Album Oriented Rock — FM radio format. The conventional thinking must have been: since he's the guy who came up with the format, he must know what it takes to get a product played on those stations. It was a misguided plan. The 1980 release, CIVILIAN, displayed a very streamlined version of all the elements that made Gentle Giant unique. The album was made up of shorter, less complicated songs, but radio would have nothing to do with it, and fans were left disappointed. Gentle Giant folded the tent and went home.

Derek Shulman eventually found his way into a successful career as a major record label executive. As Vice President at Polygram, he was responsible for signing acts such as Bon Jovi, Tears for Fears and Kingdom Come. Later, as president of Atco Records, he went on to sign AC/DC, Bad Company, Pantera and many others. Ray Shulman eventually got into commercial music writing, working with many national brand advertisers and, more recently, got into music for computer games. Phil Shulman runs a gift shop in England. Gary Green lives outside of Chicago, still playing music, and John Weathers lives in Wales working as a drummer on a variety of Welsh TV soundtracks and other smaller local acts. Kerry Minnear lives in England and runs Alucard Music, which handles the legal and royalty related issues of Gentle Giant music today.

The music that Gentle Giant created was very different, even for the 70's. It contained complicated contrapuntal arrangements, dissonant instrumental voicings and incorporated even more complicated vocal arrangements as well as unusual medieval instruments. Nontheless, they won themselves a loyal fan base and played a major role in shaping a whole sub-genre for future progressive rock bands.

- º GENTLE GIANT (1970 Vertigo)
- º ACQUIRING THE TASTE (1971 Vertigo)[also released as Motive],
- º THREE FRIENDS (1972 Vertigo)
- º OCTOPUS (1973 Vertigo)

o IN A GLASS HOUSE (1973 WWA)
o THE POWER AND THE GLORY (1974 WWA)
o FREE HAND (1975 Chrysalis)
o GIANT STEPS — THE FIRST FIVE YEARS (1975 Vertigo)
o INTERVIEW (1976 Chrysalis)
o PRETENTIOUS — FOR THE SAKE OF IT (Compilation 1977 Vertigo)
o GIANT EDITS (Compilation 1977 Capitol)
o LIVE: PLAYING THE FOOL (1977 Capitol)
o THE MISSING PIECE (1977 Capitol)
o GIANT FOR A DAY (1978 Capitol)
o CIVILIAN (1980 Columbia)
o GREATEST HITS (1981 Vertigo)
o SUPERSTAR SERIES: GENTLE GIANT (Italian Compilation 1982 Superstar)
o BBC IN CONCERT: GENTLE GIANT (1994 BBC Radio)
o OUT OF THE WOODS (1995 Band of Joy)
o THE LAST STEPS (Compilation 1996 Red Steel Music)
o UNDER CONSTRUCTION (1997 Independent)
o OUT OF THE FIRE (1998 Hux Records)
o KING BISCUIT FLOWER HOUR PRESENTS: GENTLE GIANT (1998 KBFH Records)
o TOTALLY OUT OF THE WOODS (1999 Hux Records)
o UNDER CONSTRUCTION TWO (1999 Independent)

# ~ 20 ~
# Gong (France)

There are only a few bands that survived through the 60's and 70's playing psychedelic spacey music. One that comes to mind of course is Hawkwind. But if there was ever a band to best represent the more fairy tale-ish side of music based in the 60's, it would have to be Gong. The self-proclaimed masters of pothead pixies continue to make music to this day.

For the full story we need to go back to 1967 where Daevid Allen appears on the first Soft Machine single *Feelin Reelin Squeelin*. It was R&B-based at the time, but that's where they started musically. The Soft Machine went on a small European tour and upon returning Allen was denied reentry and listed as an undesirable alien. He was, after all, of Australian heritage. Allen instead went to Paris with his partner / wife Gilli Smyth. There the two of them formed the first incarnation of Gong in late 1967.

At the time they were playing a largely improvisational style. The rest of the group included Don Cherry (trumpet), Loren Standlee (flute) and Daniel Laloux (bass drum, cello, etc.) This formation played a variety of affairs over the next couple years, all the while forging a Gong style of composition, although a band by that name had not actually been formed. Soon Didier Malherbe, a noted jazz musician, joined up and stayed even after Allen's departure in 1974.

The first record, released in 1970, was actually an Allen solo called MAGICK BROTHER / MYSTICK SISTER and featured Allen, Smyth, Malherbe, Burton Green (piano), Dieter Gewissler (bass) and Rachid Houari (drums.) It was a simple affair compositionally, but many of the songs proved to be stepping stones for the first official Gong release. The band performed at a music festival in Belgium and appeared on the same bill as Caravan, Soft Machine and Captain Beefheart. Still, getting regular gigs was proving to be difficult.

The first true Gong release came in 1971 entitled CAMEMBERT ELECTRIQUE with the lineup of Allen (guitar, vocals), Smyth (space whisper), Malherbe (sax, flute, vocals), Christian Tritsch (bass) and Pip Pyle (drums.) In 1971 they also created the soundtrack music to a film by Jerome Laperousez entitled CONTINENTAL CIRCUS. Soon thereafter, Pyle and Tritsch both left the band and, for a time, Allen disbanded Gong, choosing to work on some solo material. By the end of 1972 at the urging of Britain's Virgin Records, he brought the group back together and drafted in Steve Hillage (guitars), Tim Blake (synthesizers) and Francis Moze from Magma (bass) to replace Pyle and Tritsch. By this time Gong was one of the most popular avant-garde groups working in France, and this particular lineup became legendary. The album that resulted was part of a series entitled the Radio Gnome trilogy. The first LP of the trilogy was the 1973 release RADIO GNOME INVISIBLE VOLUME 1: FLYING TEAPOT. It was a science fiction fantasy story about pixies in a flying teapot from the Planet Gong. While music played an ever increasing role in their story telling, there was still room for a good dose of humour in the offbeat tale. VOLUME 2: ANGEL'S EGG followed in 1973 and VOLUME 3: YOU in 1974. By the time YOU was coming together, it was no longer just Daevid Allen's show, all band members were contributing to the material. As a result, YOU proved to be a strong musical statement for Gong.

At the end of 1974, after the release of YOU, Pierre Moerlen joined and left twice, unsure of his place in Gong. The first time he left his replacement was Bill Bruford who had just left King Crimson. The next time his replacement was Brian Davidson, ex of The Nice and Refugee. Moerlen, who upon seeing the departure of mainstays Allen, Hillage, and Blake decided that he had more to say musically, created Pierre Moerlen's Gong. He recruited Howlett, Malherbe and newcomers Patrice Lemoine (keyboards) and Jorge Pinchevesky (violin.) The album they created, SHAMAL, was produced by Pink Floyd drummer Nick Mason. True to the Gong form, further personnel upheavals resulted. Moerlen's Gong was a very different musical entity. Whereas the original band was a quirky spacey psychedelic influenced outfit, this version was solidly in the realm of percussion heavy rock / jazz fusion and even incorporated noted jazz rock guitarist Allen Holdsworth for the first album. Moerlen's Gong released a series of albums from 1976 through to 1988.

Gong is still going strong as of this writing, once again with Daevid Allen and Gilli Smyth at the helm. Their most recent tour of the United States, in 1996, included Malherbe, Pyle, and Mike Howlett. The discography is inclusive of Pierre Moerlen's Gong.

o MAGICK BROTHER / MYSTICK SISTER (1970 Byg)
o CAMEMBERT ELECTRIQUE (1971 Byg)
o CONTINENTAL CIRCUS (1971 Philips)
o THE FLYING TEAPOT (1972 Virgin)
o ANGELS EGG (1973 Virgin)
o YOU (1974 Virgin)
o SHAMAL (1975 Virgin)
o GAZEUZE [EXPRESSO] (1976 Virgin)
o LIVE ETC. (1977 Virgin)

- GONG EST MORT (1977 Tapioca)
- FLOATING ANARCHY (1977)
- EXPRESSO 2 (1978 Virgin)
- DOWNWIND (1979 Arista)
- TIME IS THE KEY (1979 Arista)
- P. MOERLEN'S GONG LIVE (1979 Arista)
- LEAVE IT OPEN (1980 Arista)
- RADIO GONG PT. 1 (1984 Virgin)
- RADIO GONG PT. 2 (1984 Virgin)
- THE OWL AND THE TREE (1986)
- BREAKTHROUGH (1986)
- SECOND WIND (1988)
- THE HISTORY & MYSTERY OF PLANET GONG (1990)
- GONG LIVE ON TV (1990)
- LIVE AT BATACLAN 73 (1990)
- LIVE AT SHEFFIELD 1974 (1990)
- JE N'FUME PAS DE BANANES (1992)
- SHAPESHIFTER (1992)
- CAMEMBERT ECLECTIQUE (1995)
- THE BIRTHDAY PARTY: OCT. 8TH, 9TH 1994 (1995)
- THE PEEL SESSIONS 1971-1974 (1996)
- PRE-MODERNIST WIRELESS [early BBC sessions] (1996)

# ~ 21 ~

# Grobschnitt (Germany)

While not as well known as some of the other progressive rock bands listed here, Grobschnitt have established themselves well in the world of symphonic rock. In particular, the group made quite an impact on the live scene with their wacky stage shows, which included hour long, spacey jam sessions, a multitude of interesting cabaret and slapstick interludes, innovative staging and pyrotechnics. The icing on the cake was that all the musicians and roadies used fantasy names, and all were involved in the stage show.

The band originally went by the name Kapelle Elias Grobschnitt and were from Hagen, Germany. Formed in 1970, they were one of the first acts signed to the progressive Brain label, who immediately shorted the band's name to simply Grobschnitt. Grobschnitt's self-titled debut album was recorded in the spring of

1972 in Hamburg. The recording's opening track, *Symphony*, which had been around for a couple of years, bore all the hallmarks of a multi-part symphonic prog classic and even included a string quartet from the Hamburg State Opera. Other tracks still displayed the band's penchant for long and improvised psychedelic jam sessions. The lineup at that time consisted of Eroc (drums), Alex Harlos (drums), Stefan Danielak (guitar), Bernhard Uhlemann (bass), Lupo (guitar) and Hermann Quetting (keyboards.) At the request of their record label, the band let Harlos and Quetting go and released BALLERMANN in 1974.

For their next studio effort Grobschnitt recorded JUMBO from May to June 1974. The material shows a shift in direction to an even more symphonic style due to the influence of new keyboardist Volker Kahrs. Kahrs had joined Grobschnitt in 1973, bringing with him a style of composing similar to that of Yes and Genesis. The songs on the new album were once again written by all band members together, but under the overall control of Kahrs and guitarist Lupo. In the time-honoured tradition of many progressive rock bands, they developed the music first before working on the lyrics, which were in English. Five months after the release of the English album, Grobschnitt released a new version of JUMBO with German lyrics.

It took Grobschnitt more than ten months to complete their next monumental epic, ROCKPOMMEL'S LAND, a concept album revolving around a little boy who runs away from home looking for adventure in a fantasy world. The band went into the studio well prepared because every little detail of the four songs had to be just perfect. The symphonic style of the new material was proving popular with fans, but didn't sit well with Eroc, who felt that the music was getting too complicated and arranged. Just like its predecessor, ROCKPOMMEL'S LAND was recorded at Conny Plank's Studio in Neunkirchen. In the summer of 1978, SOLAR MUSIC was released. This was the band's first live album and featured only one composition, their classic *Solar Music*. The song had originally appeared on their first album as *Sun Trip* and was then developed further as *Solar Music* for the band's second studio recording BALLERMANN. Over the years, *Solar Music* became the highlight of the Grobschnitt live experience, not only because of the music, but because of the opulent stage show surrounding it. The structure of the song allowed for endless improvising by the musicians and it's doubtful they've ever played the song the same way twice.

Their next studio effort, MERRY-GO-ROUND, was the first album produced without the help of Plank. Having perfected their art rock à la Genesis or Yes on albums like JUMBO and ROCKPOMMEL'S LAND, Grobschnitt returned to arrangements that were lighter and catchier. In many respects MERRY-GO-ROUND combined the progressive elements of the past with the immense tension of the *Solar Music* spectacle.

John Petrucci and Mike Portnoy of Dream Theater. Copyright 1999 Julie Wilson / I S Entertainment.

Phil Collins (Genesis.) Copyright 1980 Phil Anderson / KAOS2000 Magazine

Mike Rutherford (Genesis.) Copyright 1984 Phil Anderson / KAOS2000 Magazine

Ian Anderson (Jethro Tull.) Copyright Rock Classics

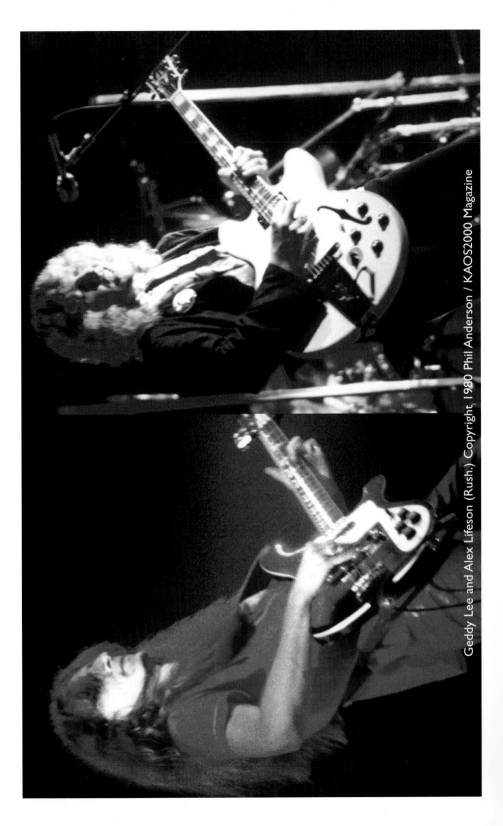

Geddy Lee and Alex Lifeson (Rush.) Copyright 1980 Phil Anderson / KAOS2000 Magazine

Steve Howe, then and now (Yes.) Copyright 1980 Phil Anderson / KAOS2000 Magazine (left) and 1999 Julie Wilson / I S Entertainment

Chris Squire (left) ... lon Anderson (Yes.) Copyright 1999 Julie Wilson / I S Entertainment

As with many prog bands, Grobschnitt changed their musical direction in the early 1980's, partially as a reaction to the influence of their new bass player Milla Kapolke. Beginning with ILLEGAL and RAZZIA *(Raid)*, they began composing shorter more commercial songs that contained less progressive rock elements and had more in common with the German new wave music of the day. Founding member Joachim 'Eroc' Ehrig left the band in the summer of 1983, but Grobschnitt continued and released the records KINDER UND NARREN *(Children And Fools)* (1984), SONNENTANZ *(Sundance)* (1985), FANTASTEN (1987) and LAST PARTY (1989).

Grobschnitt eventually sold more than 100,000 units of ROCKPOMMEL'S LAND, SOLAR MUSIC and ILLEGAL — an impressive figure for any progressive rock band. On December 6, 1989, after 19 years, 14 records and 1,356 concerts, Grobschnitt performed their farewell concert in Hagen. They are still fondly remembered today and maintain a presence on the German music scene many years after their retirement.

- o GROBSCHNITT (1972 Brain Metronome)
- o BALLERMANN (1974 Brain Metronome)
- o JUMBO (1975 Brain Metronome)
- o ROCKPOMMEL'S LAND (1977 Brain Metronome)
- o SOLAR MUSIC LIVE (1978 Brain Metronome)
- o MERRY-GO-ROUND (1979 Brain Metronome)
- o VOLLE MOLLE (1980 Brain Metronome)
- o ILLEGAL (1981 Brain Metronome)

- RAZZIA (1982 Brain Metronome)
- KINDER UND NARREN (1984 Brain Metronome)
- SONNENTANZ LIVE (1985 Brain Metronome)
- FANTASTEN (1987 Teldec)
- LAST PARTY LIVE (1990 Brain Metronome)
- DIE GROBSCHNITT — STORY ONE (1994 Metronome)
- DIE GROBSCHNITT — STORY TWO (1998 Metronome)

# ~ 22 ~
# Gryphon (England)

Progressive rock music is often noted for the manor in which it incorporates other musical genres, such as classical, jazz and avant-garde. Often missed in this melting-pot of musical ideas is folk, or more specifically in the case of Gryphon, medieval folk. This superb and often overlooked band was created in 1972 by Richard Harvey (recorders, krumhorns, glockenspiel) and Brian Gulland (bassoon, krumhorns.) Both had attended The Royal College of Music and they shared a vision of creating a musical group that mixed early English medieval and traditional folk music with more contemporary rock instruments. They enlisted the help of Graeme Taylor (guitars) and David Oberle (drums.)

Their first release in 1973 entitled GRYPHON, with it's predominantly folk emphasis, did quite well on the charts given the openness for experimentation in the early 70's. The compositions are mainly covers of traditional English folk classics, but Gryphon's sound was truly unique, even for progressive rock.

In 1974 they released MIDNIGHT MUSHRUMPS, hailed by their early fans as perhaps their best work. Once again it was a mixture of contemporary and medieval folk music. At the time it was somewhat revolutionary in it's melding of musical styles. Side two of the recording featured the title track *Midnight Mushrumps* which was a side-long extended instrumental title piece commissioned by Peter Hall for a National Theatre production of The Tempest. They continued to work within the BBC community creating music for a variety of programs. There was a brief period where the BBC's fascination with their music ran so high that it was included in many radio programs and could be heard on all four BBC channels. Later in 1974, with the lineup of Harvey, Gulland, Taylor, Oberle and Philip Nestor (bass), they scaled back the folk influence somewhat and released RED QUEEN TO GRYPHON THREE. This album consists of four instrumental compositions, all in the

ten minute range, and features the perfect blend of new and old instrumentation. This is material of the highest symphonic progressive rock order with influences as diverse as Gentle Giant with their contrapuntal instrumental interplay and Yes' thematic development. Some said that they lost their early distinctiveness, yet, in retrospect, while the contemporary instruments are very present and up-front in these compositions, the krumhorns and recorders are never very far away and still very much a part of the Gryphon sound.

The band continued to work within the artistic community, writing for radio and television commercials and a variety of television plays. They even found time to go on the road as a support act for the 1974 Yes tour of Britain and America.

A slight change in personnel preceded their 1975 release of RAINDANCE with Malcolm Bennett coming in on bass and flute. With this release, vocals made a return on half of the tracks and the band had pretty much relegated the krumhorns, recorders and bassoons to secondary status as Richard Harvey concentrated more on the plethora of keyboards now under his command — everything from Mini-moogs to Mellotrons. Following this release Richard Harvey went off to record the solo effort DIVISIONS ON A GROUND.

Some consider their last release in 1977, entitled TREASON, more of a Harvey solo effort and less of a Gryphon release, although the lineup consisted of not only Harvey, but Gulland, Oberle along with David Foster (guitar), John Davie (bass) and Alex Baird (drums.) Vocals make an appearance on all tracks and the band is very polished in its performance. Had the album been released a few years earlier, there's a good chance it would have been received quite well. Unfortunately, released at the height of punk and new wave era, it was hardly noticed other than by a small but dedicated group of followers. Gryphon was dropped from the label shortly thereafter and quietly disbanded.

Gryphon comes highly recommended by fans and critics from all corners and they continue to attract new followers who discover their unique musical style. Two comprehensive anthologies have been put together called THE COLLECTION. The first features material from their first, second and fourth albums, while the second included material from all four albums plus some unreleased material. In many respects, Gryphon exemplifies just how diverse the progressive rock genre truly is.

- GRYPHON (1973 Transatlantic)
- MIDNIGHT MUSHRUMPS (1974 Transatlantic)
- RED QUEEN TO GRYPHON THREE (1974 Transatlantic)
- RAINDANCE (1975 Transatlantic)
- TREASON (1977 Harvest)
- THE COLLECTION (1991 Progressive International)
- THE COLLECTION II (1993 Progressive International)

# ~ **23** ~

# Happy The Man (United States)

Happy The Man has been described as one of the best U.S. symphonic progressive rock groups of the mid-70's. The band was from Harrisonburg, Virginia and had formed in 1972 at the local University. Their sound was influenced by the Canterburian side of progressive rock featuring mostly instrumental compositions that managed to avoid the dissonant excesses of bands striving for complexity. Instead, Happy The Man incorporated the melodic style of Yes along with the musical complexity of Gentle Giant. Their material was full of well crafted tempo changes as the band maneuvered from 11/8 to 4/4 to and back to 5/8 time. Happy The Man embodied the virtuosic element of progressive rock.

They took their name from Goethe's book *Faust*, where many phrases begin with the line: "Happy the man who ...". As might be expected, the band members were influenced by a wide range of musical styles, including progressive rock, jazz and classical. The initial lineup consisted of Kit Watkins (keyboards), Frank Wyatt (keyboards/saxes), Stan Whitaker (guitars), Rick Kennel (bass), Mike Beck (drums/percussion) and Cliff Fortney (flute/keyboards/vocals.) Fortney soon left the band. Being the vocalist, his departure prompted the others to focus on more instrumental material.

In their early years they spent most of their time in the studio, but every once in a while they would venture out on campus for a rare gig. These live performances never failed to generate positive response and their fan base grew. In 1975 they moved to the Washington DC area, a move that proved to be very beneficial, to not only the band's mental state, but to their creative one as well. Washington was home to radio station WGTB, at the time one the country's more musically open-minded and adventurous radio outlets. It was a station not afraid to air a new band with a new sound. As a result, Happy The Man tapes benefited from a lot of airplay. Here, unlike in their hometown of Harrisonburg, the band gigged often, and it wasn't long before they developed quite a substantial following. In not too short a time, they came to the attention of Arista Record's Clive Davis, who signed them to a multi-album contract. To the record company's credit, no expense was spared on the production side. Their first two albums — HAPPY THE MAN and CRAFTY HANDS — were engineered and produced by Ken Scott, who'd established quite a reputation for himself working with Mahavishnu Orchestra and, most notably, Supertramp. As expected, the band

toured heavily in support of each disc. They were the opening act for headliners such as Renaissance and Foreigner. For their second release, Mike Beck was replaced by Ron Riddle on Drums and percussion. CRAFTY HANDS showcased the band at their best, with well crafted complex, time signatures and uniquely quirky melodies, but it came during the much simpler musical period of new wave. Sales for both albums didn't match the label's expectations and Arista dropped the band in 1978.

Returning to the studio they recorded material for a third album with yet another drummer, Coco Roussel. However, without a label, the compositions just sat on tape and shortly thereafter the band decided to split up. Kit Watkins went on to fill the keyboard slot with Camel in 1979 for a couple years before launching a very successful and prolific independent solo career. Fortunately, the demo material they had been working on eventually made it's way to vinyl and became BETTER LATE ..., released in 1979.

Nothing more was heard from Happy The Man for many years. However, interest in their limited catalogue continued to grow. This loyal following's interest didn't go unnoticed by the folks at Cuneiform Records. They eventually re-released the first three albums on CD and then added to the catalogue by releasing BEGINNINGS which features recordings made prior to their Arista signing and LIVE consisting of concert performances from 1978, all of which met critical and fan acclaim. Their most recent release, entitled DEATH'S CROWN, was composed and performed in late 1974 in Harrisonburg, before the band made the move to Washington DC, and was intended as a full multimedia, event with dancers, special lighting, slides and even actors. Fans of the band took heart in mid-1998 as rumours of a possible reunion flew across the internet. And in fact, the band spent much of late 1998 and early 1999 working towards that end.

Happy The Man maintain a soft spot in the heart of many American prog fans. This band was one of the few to challenge the musical trends of the late 70's. They were a prog band with a major label deal during the waning years of progressive rock's major label acceptance and then denial. They are considered by many to be one of America's most accomplished and influential progressive rock bands.

- o  HAPPY THE MAN (1977 Arista)
- o  CRAFTY HANDS (1978 Arista)
- o  BETTER LATE ... (1983 Cuneiform)
- o  BEGINNINGS (1992 Cuneiform)
- o  LIVE (1997 Cuneiform)
- o  DEATH'S CROWN (1999 Cuneiform)

# ~ 24 ~
# Hawkwind (England)

Hawkwind, and to a lessor degree Gong, have attained mythological status among the followers of the space-rock genre. Their fans are rabid in their dedication and, in the 90's, cross all age barriers. Hawkwind was born in late 1969, spearheaded by Dave Brock along with Mick Slattery, John Harrison, Terry Ellis (drums) and Nik Turner (saxophone.)

They were a common sight at many of the free festivals going on at the time, but perhaps the one event that brought them to prominence was the Isle of Wight Festival in 1970. The band wasn't on the bill, but they performed just the same, outside the festival fence, and what's more, they played for free. As a matter of fact, they had already built a cult following by playing just about anywhere for free. Their reputation was growing, not only for their spacey-underground style of music, but also for some well covered drug busts. Musically, Hawkwind was led by Dave Brock and Nik Turner and from the very start they specialized in long, spacey, improvisational jams, a mix of psychedelic and acid rock. But from their beginnings as a loose "collection of freaks", the band quickly began putting their interest in science fiction to music and developed a series of sci-fi themed musical masterpieces.

In 1971 they came into contact with Robert Calvert and together they released IN SEARCH OF SPACE. The music, along with the unique packaging, drew more fans to their fold. With LP titles such as IN SEARCH OF SPACE, SPACE RITUAL LIVE and WARRIOR ON THE EDGE OF TIME, they clearly positioned themselves as space-rock aficionados. While Hawkwind was more on the fringe of the symphonic progressive scene, they performed many times on the same bill with many who were an integral part of it, including Genesis. A series of profitable tours ensued and by 1974 they were ready to travel to America.

Around this time Robert Calvert left to develop a solo career. This might have been a terrible blow if not for the fact that the band began working with noted science fiction author Michael Moorcock, whose writing talents helped craft lyrical concepts in keeping with their legendary spacey music. In 1975 they recorded WARRIOR ON THE EDGE OF TIME and proceeded to tour Canada and the U.S. once more to follow up on the success of the previous year's adventure. By 1976 Hawkwind were riding high, Robert Calvert rejoined after recording a second solo record. Together with Dave Brock, Nik Turner, Simon King, Alan Powel, Simon House and Paul Rudolph they recorded ASTOUNDING SOUNDS, AMAZING MUSIC. However, it was after the next tour when things began to crumble.

First to leave was Nik Turner, then Powell, then Rudolph. The next few years were ones of even more personnel turmoil as musicians came and went. Through it all, albums were still finding their way to record shelves, all under the careful direction of Dave Brock. But the 1978 tour proved to be the final blow. As tensions mounted, Simon House left and at the end of the tour the story is told that Brock sold his guitar to a fan and was about ready to call it a day.

For a time legal issues prevented Brock from using the name Hawkwind, but in its place he returned to the studio under the name Hawklords. More recordings were undertaken and, by the early 1980's, the Hawkwind name was back in use. Around this time, Hawkwind's sound took on a little more of a heavy-metal edge as reflected in releases such as LEVITATION and SONIC ATTACK. Through much of the 80's and 90's the band carried on as they always had, new members joined and left, while original members rejoined as well. For a time during the mid-90's they existed as a trio, Dave Brock, Alan Davey, and Richard Chadwick. Throughout these years they continued to be very prolific as their discography attests.

By the late 90's, Brock had once again expanded the lineup to include a dedicated

vocalist and another guitar player. At last count Hawkwind had gone through 48 members since 1970, rivaling Gong and Soft Machine for turnover. Hawkwind's influence in the world of progressive rock has a lot to do with their perseverance, but also lies in their ability to have survived and transcended so many musical fads. Over the years they've adapted only the elements needed to continue developing their own unique space-rock style.

- HAWKWIND (1970 Liberty/UA)
- IN SEARCH OF SPACE (1971 UA)
- DOREMI FARSOL LATIDO (1972 UA)
- SPACE RITUAL (1973 Liberty UA)
- HALL OF THE MOUNTAIN GRILL (1974 UA)
- WARRIOR ON THE EDGE OF TIME (1975 UA)
- ROAD HAWKS (1976 UA)
- MASTERS OF THE UNIVERSE (1977 UA Compilation)
- QUARK STRANGENESS AND CHARM (1977 Charisma)
- PXR5 (1978 Charisma)
- HAWKLORDS (1978 Charisma)
- LIVE '79 (1979 Bronze)
- REPEAT PERFORMANCE (1979 Compilation)
- LEVITATION (1980 Bronze)
- SONIC ATTACK (1981 RCA)

o CHURCH OF HAWKWIND (1982 RCA)
o CHOOSE YOUR MASQUES (1982 RCA)
o FRIENDS AND RELATIONS (1982 Flicknife)
o FRIENDS AND RELATIONS II (1983 Flicknife)
o Zones (1983 Flicknife)
o THE TEXT OF FESTIVAL: LIVE 1970-72 (1983 Illuminated/DemiMonde)
o STONEHENGE (THIS IS HAWKWIND / DO NOT PANIC) (1984 Flicknife)
o FRIENDS AND RELATIONS III (1985)
o UTOPIA 1984 (1984 Mausoleum Compilation)
o BRING ME THE HEARD OF YURI GARAGIN (1985 DemiMonde)
o SPACE RITUAL II (1985, American Phonograph)
o LIVE '70/73 (1985 Castle Dojo)
o THE CHRONICLE OF THE BLACK SWORD (1985 Flicknife)
o ANGELS OF DEATH (1986 RCA Compilation)
o THE APPROVED HISTORY OF HAWKWIND (1986 Samurai Records)
o LIVE CHRONICLES (1986 GWR)
o OUT AND INTAKE (1987 Flicknife)
o SPIRIT OF THE AGE: THE CHARISMA YEARS (1988 Virgin)
o THE XENON CODEX (1988 GWR)
o BEST OF HAWKWIND FRIENDS & RELATIONS (1988 Flicknife)
o NIGHT OF THE HAWK (1989 Powerhouse Compilation)
o SPACE BANDITS (1990GWR)
o ACID DAZE (1990)
o STASIS — THE U.A. YEARS 1971-1975 (1990 EMI)
o PALACE SPRINGS (1991 GWR)
o THE NEVER-ENDING STORY OF THE PSYCHEDELIC WARLORDS (1991)
o HAWKWIND ANTHOLOGY (1991 Castle Communications)
o ELECTRIC TEPEE (1992 GWR/Griffin)
o THE HAWKLORDS LIVE (1992 Griffin)
o TALES FROM ATOM HENG (1992 Virgin)
o PSYCHEDELIC WARLORDS (1992 Griffin)
o CALIFORNIA BRAINSTORM (1992 Iloki)
o THE BEST OF HAWKWIND FRIENDS AND RELATIONS CD (1993 Anagram)
o UNDISCLOSED FILES (1993 Live 1984 & 1989)
o LORD OF LIGHT (1993 Griffin)
o IT IS THE BUSINESS OF THE FUTURE TO BE DANGEROUS (1993 Castle)
o THE BUSINESS TRIP (1994 EBS)
o 25 YEARS ON (1994 Gopaco)
o PSYCHEDELIC WARRIORS — THE WHITE ZONE (1995 Griffin)
o HAWKWIND FRIENDS AND RELATIONS — THE RARITIES CD (1995 Anagram)
o UNDISCLOSED FILES ADDENDUM (1995 Griffin)
o ALIEN 4 (1995 EBS)
o LOVE IN SPACE (1996 EBS)

# ~ **25** ~

# Henry Cow (England)

Even in the non-mainstream world of progressive rock there were many who achieved superstardom. But there were others who had no designs on setting the record charts on fire with hit after hit, or having a massive fan following. Such was Henry Cow, a band more dedicated to being ideologically honest with themselves than compromising artistic values.

Henry Cow was formed by Fred Frith (guitar, violin, piano) and Tim Hodgkinson (keyboards) while attending Cambridge University in early 1968, a year noted for student unrest around the world. Added to the lineup were John Greaves (bass) and Geoff Leigh (sax.) In May of 1968 they were riding the heights of the underground scene and played support for Pink Floyd at the Architects Ball. Henry Cow was a very politically aware band with a strong sense of "making a difference" with their aggressive and intrusive music. They've been described as left-wing and anti-commercial and, as a result, the mainstream music business stayed clear of the band. It wasn't until 1971, when they played the now legendary Glastonbury Fayre, that attention was thrown their way. Before this event, and even after to a certain degree, the band concentrated on smaller concerts with little if any admission price as a point of principle. Preaching their vision was more important, and in a short time they enlisted a small but fanatical following who shared similar ideological leanings.

In 1972 Chris Cutler (drums) joined the band and they began a series of concerts in London under the banner "Cabaret Voltaire" playing to individuals who enjoyed music on the fringe. Their debut album in 1973, LEGEND, was released on the foremost avant-garde label in England at the time, Virgin Records. The recording was warmly received by the small group of fans and critics alike.

In 1974 they went on a European tour supporting Captain Beefheart, then lost saxophonist Geoff Leigh but gained Lindsay Cooper. That year saw the release of UNREST. The group kept busy, with Frith releasing a solo album featuring his guitar work and then proceeded to pen a series of articles on guitar technique in one of the British music papers. Henry Cow also began working with label-mates Slapp Happy. While their musical styles were not all that similar, the blending of the two groups produced the 1975 recording DESPERATE STRAIGHTS and it too garnered critical acclaim. The association seemed to work and together they planned for a follow-up release, which appeared in late 1975. IN PRAISE OF

LEARNING resulted in members of Slapp Happy departing, other than vocalist Dagmar Krause who stayed on with Henry Cow. Following this release, over the next two years, the band undertook some serious touring throughout much of Britain and the European continent.

The term used to describe Henry Cow's musical style within the prog community is Rock In Opposition, or RIO for short, and it's even used to describe a number of bands working in a similar musical style such as Univers Zero and Art Zoyd. Yet, interestingly enough, the term RIO wasn't intended to describe a musical style as much as it was to describe bands with a similar ideological position as it related to the music business. In 1978 Henry Cow released WESTERN CULTURE, and then later that year ceased to exist. While touring in Europe they met up with a number of other bands who, like Cow, were working on the fringes of mainstream music and not getting any recognition from the major labels. Out of this closed door policy, Cutler and Henry Cow created a touring festival and called it RIO, or Rock In Opposition, to get noticed by the media. They got noticed and the term caught on. By late 1979, divorced from it's original intent of marketing the music and concerts, the term took on a meaning all it's own and to this day continues to be applied to bands who work in a politicized avant-garde direction.

The music of Henry Cow displayed influences from Soft Machine, Frank Zappa and Kurt Weill but, while they incorporated these influences, the music they created was entirely unique; a strange blend of intricate structure and improvisation that few have ever matched — adventurous and challenging to listen to. Throughout their time as Henry Cow and in the solo efforts which followed, the members remained firmly committed to their ideological or political cause. They were and remain one of the most experimental progressive rock bands. Their dedication didn't bring them a massive following, but they did achieve a dedicated core of fans, particularly in Europe. Over the years the original members have continued to work together, mostly at the direction of Cutler in a variety of loose musical associations.

- o LEGEND (1973 Virgin)
- o UNREST (1974 Virgin)
- o DESPERATE STRAIGHTS (1975 Virgin)
- o IN PRAISE OF LEARNING (1975 Virgin)
- o HENRY COW CONCERTS (1976 Caroline)
- o WESTERN CULTURE (1978 Recommended)

# ~ **26** ~

# IQ (England)

In the early eighties, during the progressive rock revival that took place in England, three bands quickly came to the forefront: Marillion, Pallas and IQ. IQ were the last to secure a major label recording contract which, at the time, was seen to be the only way to success. The independent label distribution network was nowhere near as developed as it is today.

IQ's history goes back to 1976 and a band called The Lens. The Lens went through various personnel changes but survived until July of 1981, at which time guitarist Mike Holmes and keyboardist Martin Orford continued on as IQ. Later, in June of 1982, Peter Nicholls joined as vocalist. By this time the band had moved to London. Shortly after this, their first cassette album, SEVEN STORIES INTO EIGHT, was released. The cassette unashamedly displayed their progressive rock roots, with its complex time changes, shifting moods and influences from Camel to Genesis. What followed was a lot of hard work, composing new material and performing on the road, including their first appearance at The Marquee in September of 1982. Major exposure came when they opened for The Enid on a number of dates. All this activity culminated in September 1983 with a headlining appearance at The Marquee and the simultaneous release of their first vinyl LP, TALES FROM THE LUSH ATTIC. It was a smashing success for IQ and the fledgling neo-progressive rock movement.

In 1985 IQ released one of the best neo-progressive LP's of the 80's — THE WAKE. The group went on an exhaustive tour with Wishbone Ash, which culminated with a performance at London's Hammersmith Odeon. The torturous touring caused friction within the group and lead vocalist Peter Nicholls left. Undaunted, IQ recruited new vocalist Paul Menel. In 1986 they played London's Piccadilly Theatre and their performance led to a lucrative deal with Phonogram records. The band's third studio album, NOMZAMO, was released in 1987 and showed them moving in a more commercial direction. That same year they also performed in Europe for the first time. For their next album, ARE YOU SITTING COMFORTABLY, the group was produced by Terry Brown, noted for his work with Rush. Once again the band was incorporating a more commercial sound. This release was followed by a full European tour in support of Mike and the Mechanics.

1990 was a pivotal year for IQ. Internally there was dissatisfaction over musical

direction, which resulted in Paul Menel (vocals) and Tim Esau (bass) leaving the group. In addition, the band felt that they weren't getting support from the record company, which became moot when their label Squawk folded. IQ was left with a choice of looking for another label or going the independent route again. Peter Nicholls was asked to fill in temporarily, along with original Lens bassist Les Marshall. However, after only two performances, Marshall died suddenly and unexpectedly. Once again the band was at a crossroads. Marshall's death brought the members together. Nicholls buoyed by the two live performances felt new inspiration and decided to stay on. The band brought in new bassist John Jowitt, formerly of Ark, and started their own label Giant Electric Pea.

IQ made their American debut at Progfest 93 in Los Angeles and performed new material from their forthcoming CD EVER. It was such a strong comeback release that IQ was winning accolades from audiences in America, Europe and Britain. EVER marked a return to the progressive sound of the old IQ. Aided by superior musicianship as a result of their touring and by heightened production values, EVER became yet another landmark for IQ and the new and growing prog rock underground. IQ returned to America in 1994 as well as touring extensively in Europe. Simultaneously they won back the rights to their earlier releases and set about repackaging them for re-release on their own label. April 1996 saw the release of a live double CD and video boxed-set entitled FOREVER LIVE. It received excellent reviews, but was only a sign of things to come.

In September 1997 the progressive rock community was treated to SUBTERRANEA, the new double CD concept album, and a tour incorporating a full theatrical show. Once again the CD was received with glowing reviews and in Britain IQ cleaned up at the annual Classic Rock Society Awards by winning, Best

Album, Best Band and many of the individual musician categories.

In 1998 IQ came full circle when they went into the studio and completely re-recorded their first cassette tape, re-titling it SEVEN STORIES INTO '98. Packaged as a double CD, it contained not only the new material but a copy of the original for comparison's sake. How far the band had come!

IQ's inclusion as one of prog's 50 most influential bands, comes from having started out in the early 80's to become a prog force to be reckoned with through the 90's. Their dedication to the genre is second to none, as their late 90's releases amply demonstrate. Unlike so many bands who veer off in a more commercial direction, IQ may have experimented there, but after two LPs returned to the prog fold with renewed vigour. Their releases since have been second to none.

- o SEVEN STORIES INTO EIGHT (1982 Independent Tape)
- o TALES FROM THE LUSH ATTIC (1983 GEP)
- o THE WAKE (1985 GEP)
- o NINE IN A POUND IS HERE (1985 Semi-official Bootleg)
- o LIVING PROOF (1986 GEP)
- o NOMZAMO (1987 GEP)
- o ARE YOU SITTING COMFORTABLY (1989 GEP)
- o J'AI POLLETTE D'ARNU (1991 GEP)
- o EVER (1994 GEP)
- o FOREVER LIVE (1996 GEP)
- o SUBTERRANEA (1997 GEP)
- o SEVEN STORIES INTO 98 (1998 GEP)
- o THE LOST ATTIC (1999 GEP)

# ~ *27* ~
# Jethro Tull (England)

Jethro Tull came on the scene in early 1968 consisting of Ian Anderson (vocals, flute, guitar), Glen Cornick (bass), Mick Abrams (guitar) and Clive Bunker (drums.) As most fans know, they took their name from an 18th century agriculturist. From the very beginning, Ian Anderson's outlandish costumes and stage antics made audiences and critics take notice. Augmented by an original, breathy flute delivery, Jethro Tull quickly established itself as a force to be

copyright 1980 Phil Anderson / KAOS2000 Magazine

reckoned with.

Their first recordings were more overtly blues influenced and the subtle jazz hints made 1968's THIS WAS a standout. Shortly after it's release, a rift developed between Anderson and Abrams so Abrams left to form Blodwyn Pig. The guitarists slot was filled briefly by Tony Iommi until Martin Barre came in on a more permanent basis. No longer having to share leadership, Ian Anderson assumed control. This quickly led to their 1969 release STAND UP which contained the top five single *Living In The Past.* While blues was popular at the time, without Abrams there to champion the cause, Tull under Anderson's direction was moving further away from that style, not yet incorporating a full progressive rock stance, but getting there. The album reached the No. 1 spot on the British charts for a few weeks. During the next few months, a series of sell out performances helped the band not only define their musical direction but their stage presence as well. It was during this time that Anderson developed the whole jester / tramp / Dickens persona.

Riding on their British success, Jethro Tull hit big in the United States as well. Their third LP, 1970's BENEFIT, was a big seller in the U.S., although less so in Britain. Perhaps as a result of the band's focus on the American market, the album didn't seem to be as popular with British audiences. BENEFIT featured well developed melodic compositions aided by keyboards from John Evan. But it was 1971's AQUALUNG that solidified Jethro Tull's progressive rock direction. Evan was now a permanent fixture on keyboards and Cornick had left to be replaced by Jeffrey Hammond-Hammond. This was the first of a few concept albums for Jethro Tull, with compositions taking whole sides of approximately 20 minutes each, incorporating a mixture of electric and acoustic passages, moody dramatics and philosophical lyrics. AQUALUNG received plenty of radio airplay with songs such as *Hymn 43* and *Locomotive Breath.* Late in 1971, Clive Bunker departed leaving Anderson the only surviving founding member. Bunker's replacement was Barriemore Barlow. Jethro Tull spent a good part of 1971 and 72 touring, mostly in the United States. Picking up on the success of long form concepts, Jethro Tull released THICK AS A BRICK in 1972. This time it was one continuous piece of music spread over two sides. BRICK was originally packaged in a quasi-newspaper full of humorous stories poking fun at institutions and icons of the day. This was followed by the 1973 release of A PASSION PLAY. In Britain the press turned on Jethro Tull with the critics panning A PASSION PLAY and many writers pulling out the clichéd barbs pretentious, cold and passionless. Feeling the pressure, Jethro Tull announced their "retirement" from the concert scene. Anderson later admitted their retirement was actually a little grandstanding for the press and was also a response to feeling somewhat misunderstood. The band headed off to Switzerland to work on their next release, originally intended as a movie soundtrack, 1974's WAR CHILD. Not a concept this time, WAR CHILD instead hearkened back slightly to an earlier sound. They released *Bungle in the Jungle* which turned out to be a big hit receiving airplay across North America. The group spent a good portion of late 1974 and much of 1975 on the road performing to sell out crowds in the U.S. and UK.

copyright 1980 Phil Anderson / KAOS2000 Magazine

MINSTREL IN THE GALLERY followed up musically in 1975. Tull continued to sell better in the US although by this time Hammond-Hammond had returned to art studies and was replaced by John Glascock. Jethro Tull had firmly established a musical style that encompassed a combination of long and short songs incorporating elements of blues, jazz, folk and rock and the albums that followed through the late 70's and 80's maintained this momentum. Each time critics signaled the demise of the band, they returned with solid material. Such was the case with A in 1980 aided on keyboards and violin by ex-Curved Air member

Eddie Jobson, and then again with the solid 1995 release ROOTS TO BRANCHES. Jethro Tull spent a good portion of 1997-98 on tour around the world in support of ROOTS TO BRANCHES, again playing to sell out crowds.

In between his work with Tull and various solo projects, Ian Anderson lives on a farm in Scotland raising fish. With an extensive catalogue of fine releases Jethro Tull continues in the 90's to uphold their position as one of the "big six" in the world of progressive rock. Their most recent releases ably demonstrate their ability to craft classic prog material with a very modern sensibility.

- THIS WAS ... JETHRO TULL (1968 Reprise)
- STAND UP (1969 Reprise)
- BENEFIT (1970 Reprise)
- AQUALUNG (1971 Chrysalis)
- THICK AS A BRICK (1972 Chrysalis)
- LIVING IN THE PAST (1972 Chrysalis)
- PASSION PLAY (1973 Chrysalis)
- WAR CHILD (1974 Chrysalis)
- MINSTREL IN THE GALLERY (1975 Chrysalis)
- TOO OLD TO ROCK AND ROLL (1976 Chrysalis)
- M.U.: THE BEST OF JETHRO TULL (1976 Chrysalis)
- SONGS FROM THE WOOD (1977 Chrysalis)
- HEAVY HORSES (1978 Chrysalis)
- BURSTING OUT LIVE (1978 Chrysalis)
- STORMWATCH (1978 Chrysalis)
- A (1980 Chrysalis)
- BROADSWORD AND THE BEAST (1982 Chrysalis)
- UNDERWRAPS (1984 Chrysalis)
- CREST OF A KNAVE (1987 Chrysalis)
- 20 YEARS OF JETHRO TULL: HIGHLIGHTS (1988 Chrysalis)
- ROCK ISLAND (1989 Chrysalis)
- CATFISH RISING (1991 Chrysalis)
- A LITTLE LIGHT MUSIC (1992 Chrysalis)
- 25<sup>th</sup> ANNIVERSARY BOX SET (1993 Chrysalis)
- ROOTS TO BRANCHES (1995 Chrysalis)

# ~ **28** ~

# Kansas (United States)

By 1975 the United States was beginning to boast of its own progressive rock scene, best typified by a band from Topeka, Kansas called, naturally enough, Kansas. Kansas had spent the previous few years playing clubs and small halls. It was this incessant gigging that enabled them, like many a prog band before them, to hone their playing abilities. Towards the end of 1974, music mogul Don Kirshner heard their demo tape and signed them to his label.

The original lineup consisted of Steve Walsh (keyboards, vocals), Rich Williams (guitar), Dave Hope (bass), Kerry Livgren (guitar, keyboards), Robbie Steinhardt (violin) and Phil Ehart (drums.) Their first LP, KANSAS, was released in 1974, while 1975 saw their Anglo-symphonic progressive rock sound perfected in SONG FOR AMERICA and MASQUE. In 1976 came LEFTOVERTURE and their first mega hit from the pen of Kerry Livgren, *Carry on Wayward Son*. It was at the peak of the so-called arena rock period and radio was in its AOR — Album Oriented Rock — phase and the tune was just perfect. The touring continued unabated. Kansas was very much a road band. The album went Platinum soon after its release.

They followed up their success with POINT OF KNOW RETURN and another giant hit ballad from Livgren entitled *Dust in the Wind*. By this time Kansas was being solidly compared with their progressive rock counterparts in Britain. The band was crafting long compositions, including a feisty violin with loads of keyboards, and mixing it up with some American-style drumming and guitar work. Add to this the striking LP packaging and Kansas was proving to be a fine blend of some of the best Anglo and American prog with a certain accessibility as demonstrated on the next few releases. That accessibility became an issue for Steve Walsh who wanted to concentrate on a harder edged rock sound. Concerned with the band's drift towards a more commercial sound, he left after 1980's AUDIO VISIONS and was replaced on vocals for the next two releases, VINYL CONFESSIONS and DRASTIC MEASURES, by John Elefante. By this time the band had settled into creating music that fell into the three to four minute range with little of their early adventurousness. This was compounded by the departure of violinist Robbie Steinhardt after VINYL CONFESSIONS.

Kansas officially split in 1983 when both Livgren and Hope left to pursue careers in Christian music with a progressive rock edge. Kansas ceased to exist for about two years. Then, in 1986, Kansas became Ehart and Williams, with a returned

Steve Walsh, and they added Billy Greer on bass and Steve Morse from the Dixie Dregs on guitar. This formation released POWER, produced by Andrew Powell of Alan Parsons fame. While it was no return to the glory days, POWER did have its share of interesting compositions and arrangements. The lineup stayed the same for the next release in 1988, IN THE SPIRIT OF THINGS, produced by Bob Ezrin, noted for his work with Alice Cooper and Pink Floyd. Ezrin brings his trademark sound to Kansas with a larger than life orchestration providing a solid backdrop for one of their more mysterious releases. Then Kansas split up again.

Four years passed before a promoter arranged for a small tour in Germany and the band reformed with the original members except Steinhardt. It wasn't to last and after a short time Livgren and Hope departed again. The rest of Kansas brought in David Ragsdale (violin) in 1991, and continued to play live, releasing LIVE AT THE WHISKY in 1992. Gone were the large arenas, now it was back to where they'd begun, the smaller halls and clubs.

They surprised everyone in 1995 with FREAKS OF NATURE. This release was a welcome return to a more adventurous compositional style, linking songs together, orchestration and even a ballad from Kerry Livgren thrown it. FREAKS OF NATURE was a powerful return. The band went on one of their trademark tours through 1996 and 97 in support of Styx, playing to larger halls filled to capacity.

Ragsdale, who'd been brought in as a hired-hand, left to concentrate on solo work, at which point they chose to bring Robbie Steinhardt back into the group. After a number of albums, keyboardist Greg Roberts left to spend more time with his family, leaving the group as Ehart, Walsh, Williams, Greer and Steinhardt. They took off to London to perform a live concert with the London Symphony

Orchestra. A variety of their older classic numbers and three new ones came to be their next release entitled ALWAYS NEVER THE SAME in 1998.

For many, Kansas became the American counterpart to bands like Yes and Genesis. Kansas continues to craft their style of progressive rock through their many albums to great effect. They even came up with a couple of hits along the way. Their early material featured the violin up front, while their middle period material became more guitar oriented, only to see the return of the distinctive violin during the 90's. For some fans, it's the early long epics, for others it's the newer, dynamic shorter compositions. Whichever you choose, Kansas continues to add to their musical legacy.

- o KANSAS (1974 Kirshner)
- o MASQUE (1975 Kirshner)
- o SONG FOR AMERICA (1975 Kirshner)
- o LEFTOVERTURE (1975 Kirshner)
- o POINT OF KNOW RETURN (1978 Kirshner)
- o TWO FOR THE SHOW (1978 Kirshner)
- o MONOLITH (1979 Kirshner)
- o AUDIO VISIONS (1980 Kirshner)
- o VINYL CONFESSIONS (1982 Kirshner)
- o DRASTIC MEASURES (1983 CBS)
- o THE BEST OF KANSAS (1984 Epic)
- o POWER (1986 MCA)
- o IN THE SPIRIT OF THINGS (1988 MCA)
- o CARRY ON (Compilation 1990 CBS)
- o LIVE AT THE WHISKY (1992 Intersound)
- o KANSAS: BOX SET (1994 Epic)
- o FREAKS OF NATURE (1995 Intersound)
- o KING BISCUIT FLOWER HOUR PRESENTS: KANSAS (1998 King Biscuit Music)
- o ALWAYS NEVER THE SAME (1998 River North)
- o BEST OF KANSAS (Revised 1999 Sony)

# ~ 29 ~

# King Crimson (England)

The first point that needs to be made is that King Crimson did not create the first the first progressive rock recording. However, their legacy to the genre is that their appearance on the scene ensured that progressive rock was not only to become a viable musical genre, but that it was also a fashionable one as well — fashionable in the sense that people started taking it seriously.

The roots of King Crimson start pre-1969 with the light weight pop effort GILES, GILES & FRIPP. After failing to get any gigs whatsoever, and receiving dismal response from anyone who heard them, Pete Giles left. Around the end of 1968, Pete's brother Mike (drums) and Robert Fripp (guitar, Mellotron) conceived of King Crimson and added Ian McDonald (reeds) and Greg Lake (bass, vocals) and King Crimson was born. Interestingly, while they were honing their chops in various London clubs and cafes, one evening Justin Hayward and Graeme Edge of The Moody Blues came by to listen and briefly considered signing them to their newly formed Threshold label. The smaller gigs started happening, but in July of 1969 King Crimson secured a spot on the Rolling Stones free concert in Hyde Park, playing before an estimated 650,000 people. Their use of Mellotrons and classical influences mesmerized the crowd.

In October 1969 they released their first LP, IN THE COURT OF THE CRIMSON KING, to almost unanimous critical approval. In typical rock fashion, Mike Giles departed following the band's first tour of America. Now as a trio, King Crimson commenced working on their second release, IN THE WAKE OF POSEIDON, only to have Greg Lake leave to form Emerson Lake & Palmer. Gordon Haskell came in to complete the vocals and Pete Giles returned on bass. The search was on for a drummer. In late 1970 the new lineup of King Crimson was Fripp, Haskell, Mel Collins (reeds) Andy McCulloch (drums) and Pete Sinfield (lyrics.) With this group and a host of guest musicians they released LIZARD in December 1970. A few days after its release Haskell was let go.

A revised lineup of Fripp, Collins, Sinfield (keyboards) Ian Wallace (drums) and unknown Boz Burrell (bass, vocals) charged ahead. They recorded ISLANDS in 1971, after which they returned to tour the U.S. For a variety of reasons, both musical and personal, this lineup met the same fate as the last to tour, they fell apart. The tour hadn't really gone that well either. The U.S. crowds wanted to hear the early material and Fripp was more interested in presenting the new compositions. Totally disillusioned, he returned to England, spending time in seclusion and pondering the fate of King Crimson.

The new line up proved to be a good one with Fripp adding Bill Bruford (drums), John Wetton (bass, vocals), Jamie Muir (percussion) and David Cross (violin, Mellotron.) King Crimson went from strength to strength with this powerful lineup, some say the best, releasing LARKS TONGUE IN ASPIC in 1973. With Muir's departure, the band, now a quartet, created STARLESS AND BIBLE BLACK the following year, after which Cross departed. After yet another U.S. tour the band returned to England where Fripp promptly announced the dissolution of King Crimson. They posthumously released RED to even more critical acclaim. RED was probably the most aggressive to date and would prove to be a strong influence for a host of new progressive rock bands in the 90's.

A new styled King Crimson appeared on the scene in 1981. This time reflecting a totally different musical approach and, while Fripp decried the progressive rock tag, many of his followers continued to see the band within the genre. With Adrian Belew along side, this edition of King Crimson was even harder edged still. They eventually released three recordings: DISCIPLINE, BEAT and THREE OF A PERFECT PAIR, and undertook a number of well received concert tours. Some critics accused the third release of self-parody but from Fripp's standpoint it was mission accomplished as he again disbanded King Crimson.

This time the self imposed exile lasted for a decade, King Crimson returned in 1995 with yet another new sound, this time incorporating the latest technological gizmos to produce guitar dominated, dense sonic textures. The band played a sold out U.S. tour and continued to win the praise of fans and critics.

Fripp has always been the heart of King Crimson — a role he has assumed sometimes grudgingly. Over the years he has more than once berated fans and critics for their views and yet the near obsequious fan support has always been there. Also, over the years, Fripp has attempted to, not too successfully, distance himself and his efforts from the prog community. One of his ongoing projects has been to release live material from every incarnation of the band, a project which is virtually complete. King Crimson's creative vision gave progressive rock the credibility to gel as a genre and for that they can never be thanked enough.

o  IN THE COURT OF THE CRIMSON KING (1969 Atlantic)
o  IN THE WAKE OF POSEIDON (1970 Atlantic)
o  LIZARD (1970 Atlantic)
o  ISLANDS (1971 Atlantic)
o  EARTHBOUND (1972 Island)

- LARK'S TONGUES IN ASPIC (1973 Atlantic)
- STARLESS AND BIBLE BLACK (1974 Atlantic)
- RED (1974 Atlantic)
- USA (1975 Atlantic)
- A YOUNG PERSON'S GUIDE TO KING CRIMSON (1975 Island)
- DISCIPLINE (1981 EG)
- BEAT (1982 EG)
- 3 OF A PERFECT PAIR (1984 Warner Brothers)
- ESSENTIAL KING CRIMSON (1991 Caroline)
- FRAME BY FRAME (1991 Caroline Compilation)
- THE GREAT DECEIVER [RECORDED 1973-74] (1992)
- VROOM (1994)
- THRAK (1995)
- B'BOOM — LIVE IN ARGENTINA (1996)
- THRAKATTAK (1996)
- THE NIGHTWATCH [RECORDED 1973] (1998)

# ~ 30 ~
# Le Orme (Italy)

Just as there exist the "big six" British progressive rock bands, there is also the "big three" based in Italy, namely Banco, PFM and Le Orme. Le Orme were noted for creating beautiful melodies in songs and concept albums. They were also tagged with ELP comparisons, although the two have little in common musically. If anything, the comparison was drawn because of the instrumentation and trio nature of the group.

The band's roots go back as far as 1967 releasing singles and an album of what was called "beat" music. It wasn't until 1971's COLLAGE that Le Orme took the prog plunge and began to mix classical, jazz, folk and rock. The group at the time consisted of Aldo Tagliapietra (guitars, vocals), Antonio Pagliuca (keyboards) and Miki dei Rossi (percussionist.)

Maturing quickly as a result of live performances, they released UOMO DI PEZZA in 1972, an album with music that's slightly softer and more fully arranged. Later that same year Le Orme released their masterpiece, FELONA AND SORONA, featuring lyrics by Peter Hammill. It's a classic prog story line of two planets, one happy and one sad, briefly coming together only to end with both planets

destroyed. This was a continous work similar to Jethro Tull's A Passion Play which was released that same year. For a while it was the number one selling album in Italy and was created in both English and Italian versions.

Taking a break from new material, they released their first live album, IN CONCIERTO, in 1974. But before long they produced the follow-up to FELONA AND SORONA, entitled CONTRAPPUNTI, at which time producer Gian Piero

Reverberi became the fourth member as pianist. Lyrically Le Orme typify prog rock's philosophical or social conscience side. UOMO DI PEZZA dealt with the abuse of women by men, and CONTRAPPUNTI features compositions dealing with such issues as India's nuclear arms race, neglect of the poor and the horrors of back alley abortions.

During the mid-70's Le Orme began to travel and their next three albums were written and recorded outside of Italy. These albums include 1975's SMOGMAGICA (in Los Angeles), 1976's VERITA NASCOSTE (London) and 1977's STORIA O LEGGENDA (Paris.) In addition, over this time period they underwent some personnel changes. In 1975 Tolo Marton was added on lead guitar and his efforts to take the band in a rockier direction can be heard on SMOGMAGICA. In 1976 he was replaced by Germano Serafin (guitar) which resulted in a return to their vintage prog style as heard on VERITA NASCOSTE.

Their next release, in 1979 entitled FLORIAN, had the band divesting themselves of synths and electric guitars and going virtually acoustic with the addition of a selection of classical instruments. It was Le Orme "unplugged." Growing in confidence, the band experimented with more traditional classical instruments in their new compositions. The experience of using real violins showed a more mature band with the release of PICCALO RAPSODIA DELL'APE in 1980. Shortly after this release guitarist Sarafin left and Le Orme were now back to the original trio. Given the nature of pop music in the early 80's, most everyone thought that progressive rock was no longer viable and so Le Orme went for a pop sound with VENERDI in 1982. Their most commercial, this LP features short songs with traditional pop compositional arrangements.

This wasn't the way that fans wanted the band to go out, but in fact Le Orme ceased to exist for approximately three years. It wasn't until the late 80's that Le Orme reunited and toured Italy for a while and ultimately released ORME in 1990 still showing them in the pop commercial style. Then, in 1992, keyboardist Toni Pagliuca left to be replaced by two keyboardists: Francesco Sartori and Michele Bon. There was no news of Le Orme for years.

Four years later, in 1996, they took the prog community by surprise releasing IL FIUME, their first concept album since FELONA AND SORONA. This one talks about the stages of life and compares them to the flow of a river. The band was invited to perform at ProgFest 97 as headliners for the first day's performances. They were the hit of the show, wowing everyone, performing all of their current CD IL FIUME as well as the entire classic FELONA AND SORONA. The performance left no doubt that Le Orme were back.

While it looked like Le Orme were to disappear without a whimper in the early

90's, they surprised everyone by returning with a strong prog release. Le Orme were one of the first Italian bands to follow in the Anglo footsteps and they became hugely popular in Italy and Britain carving out a unique melodic style that has continued into their current recordings. They've proven to be a powerful influence on the current generation of Italian prog musicians.

o COLLAGE (1971 Philips)
o UOMO DI PEZZA (1972 Philips)
o FELONA & SORONA (1973 Philips)
o IN CONCERTO (1974 Philips)
o CONTRAPUNTI (1974 Philips)
o BEYOND LENG (1975 Cosmos)
o SMOGMAGICA (1975 Philips)
o VERITA NASCOSTE (1976 Philips)
o STORIA O LEGGENDA (1977 Philips)
o FLORIAN (1979 Philips)
o PICCALO RAPSODIA DELL' APE (1980 Philips)
o VENERDI (1981 DDD)
o ORME (1990)
o IL FIUME (1996 Tring)

# ~ 31 ~
# Magma (France)

When it comes to stretching the musical boundaries of progressive rock, one name comes quickly to mind — Magma. They were a French band fronted by Christian Vander, who took progressive rock to a completely new level — some say a new planet. Their albums wove an intricate science fiction story sung in a language created specifically for the tale. Chock full of chanting, dissonance and loud rock, this material was not for the timid. The band's stated influences included Bela Bartok, Stockhausen, Duke Ellington and blues-shouting all blended together to create a unique, adventurous form of music that was destined not to appeal to everyone. They, and bands that followed in their style, came to form the Zeuhl sub-genre of progressive music.

Formed in France in late 1969 by Vander, they came out of the vibrant French musical underground. The group consisted of many top-caliber musicians, most of whom, however, had never achieved any prominence in the press. While

Vander relied on the collective input of the other members, and sometimes those ideas were substantial, he remained the one constant. Magma was his musical vision. But more than that, it was a total concept package — the art, the music, even the newly created language to tie it all together. It was called Kobaian and served to tell the story from the beginning.

That beginning starts with the 2-record set entitled MAGMA released in 1970. The first disc tells the tale of the journey to Kobaia, while the second tells the tale of a space ship rescue. The spaceship has Earthmen aboard who request that the Kobaians come to earth and teach their philosophy and, in a sense, save the earth from itself.

Their second album, 1001 DEGREES CENTIGRADES released in 1971, picks up the story with the Kobaians' arrival on earth, where they are listened to briefly before being tossed in jail. At this point, the Kobaians back home threaten the earth with utter destruction unless they release the prisoners. After a time the authorities agree and the Kobaians leave vowing never to return. And so the story goes. The third album, MEKANIK DESTRUKTIW KOMMANDOH, picks up the story with one of the aliens' earthly converts and the tale continues until it closes with the release of 1978's ATTAHK, which turned out to be Magma's last LP to exclusively use Kobaian.

Nothing further was heard from Magma for a number of years, and it wasn't until 1984's MERCI that they returned to the recording world. This release has songs in English, French, and a couple Kobaian, but it's clear that Vander and Magma are attempting to move beyond their origins and leave Kobaia behind. Sadly for Magma fans, this turned out to be the band's final studio release for many years.

Vander continued creating music and, in an effort to discover new rhythms and thus new melodies, moved the music more into the Coltrane-inspired jazz arena. He formed a trio called Offering and toured smaller clubs in Europe and North America. Then, in the mid-90's, Vander decided to put Magma back together with a group of new musicians. Following extensive tours of Europe and Japan they returned in 1999 to tour North America for the first time in 25 years. The music for the tour consisted of selections from some of their classic early recordings as well as a couple of new pieces. Also in the works was the creation of more new material for a forthcoming CD, as well as a solo album from Vander.

Magma were very much a part of the burgeoning French prog scene on the same level as Ange and Gong. The music they created may have defied traditional classification, but there's no question that Magma were as influential as some of the more mainstream prog groups. The music of Magma straddles many genres from jazz to 20ᵗʰ Century classical composition. There are hints of Soft Machine,

early Chicago blues, lots of improvisation and even the use of the voice as an instrument. Magma's music was never for the timid, but they will forever be remembered in history as having been chiefly responsible for creating the progressive rock sub-genre of Zeuhl.

- o MAGMA (1970 Philips)
- o 1001 CENTIGRADE (1971 Philips)
- o MEKANIK KOMMANDOH (73 — released 1989)
- o MEKANIK DESTRUKTIW KOMMANDOH (1973 A&M)
- o WURDAH ITAH (1974 Soundtrack)
- o KOHNTARKOSZ (1974 A&M)
- o LIVE (1975 Utopia)
- o UDU WUDU (1976 Utopia)
- o INEDITS (1977 Tapioca)
- o ATTAHK (1978 Tomato)
- o RETROSPEKTIW III (1981 RCA)
- o RETROSPEKTIW I / II (1981 RCA)
- o CONCERT BOBINO 1981 (1981)
- o MERCI (1984)
- o MYTHES ET LEGENDES VOL. I (1985)
- o THEATRE DU TAUR CONCERT 1975 (1994)
- o MEKANIK ZEUHL WORTZ (1994)
- o CONCERT 1971 BRUXELLES - THEATRE I 40 (1996)

# ~ 32 ~
# Marillion (England)

Without question, the band most responsible for the resurgence of progressive rock during the early 80's is Marillion. It was Marillion who struck terror in the hearts of music critics in Britain in 1982 by selling out two nights at the prestigious Hammersmith Odeon on the strength of releasing only one hit single — *Market Square Heroes*. Despite all of the critic's abuse, it seemed there was an audience for progressive rock after all.

Marillion's roots go back to 1978 when drummer Mick Pointer formed a four piece instrumental group called Silmarillion. Guitarist Steve Rothery came on board in 1979, as did bassist Pete Trewavas. They gigged around their home base of Aylesbury to less than enthusiastic response. Sometime late 1980 they decided to add a vocalist. Enter Fish. The band had recorded a song called *The Web* and sent a copy to Fish. Early in 1981 Fish turned up at their doorstep with lyrics in hand and was hired shortly thereafter. By this time they had dropped the "Sil" and were just known as Marillion. After a few weeks of rehearsals they performed their first vocal gig March 1981 at the Red Lion pub in Bicester. It was around this time they sent out their first demo to promoters. It contained *He Knows You Know*, *Garden Party*, and *Charting The Single*. Later in the year they hired Keith Goodwin to be their publicist. Goodwin had done his share to help progressive rock the first time around as the publicist for Yes and ELP, among others. His experience allowed him to put the name Marillion in front of all the right people. They played live everywhere — halls, pubs, clubs, you name it, and in the process, fine tuned their music, their style, their stage show and most importantly their musicianship. Around the end of the year they were looking for a new keyboard player. They remembered seeing Mark Kelly performing with a band called Chemical Alice and he was asked to join. The lineup now being Pointer, Rothery, Kelly, Trewavas and Fish, in January of 1982 they played their first Marquee date.

By the fall of 1982 they proved to be the first of the neo-progressive rock bands to be signed to a major recording contract. It was with EMI, a company they remained with until 1996. A couple of singles were quickly released. They were voted "Best New Band of 1982" by *Sounds*. Things were going along very nicely when they released their first LP, SCRIPT FOR A JESTER'S TEAR, in March of 1983.

A series of well charting singles and albums followed in quick succession, each

doing better than the last and pushing the band to even greater prominence. In 1985 the band's third LP, MISPLACED CHILDHOOD, debuted at No. 1 in the UK charts and has since sold more than 2 million copies world wide. It was the album that was going to break Marillion as a worldwide smash. In Britain and Europe there was no question. The follow-up in 1987 was CLUTCHING AT STRAWS and it debuted at No. 2 on the charts in the UK, however recognition in the U.S. was hard to come by. In part it was this lack of international recognition that led to Fish's departure in 1988 while the band was in the midst of recording SEASONS END. His replacement was Steve Hogarth who completed the vocal work on the album. Hogarth's association with Marillion has created a very different sounding band, as they seemed to move further and further away from their prog roots. This became even more evident with the 1991 release HOLIDAYS IN EDEN.

The brightest prog spot of the post-Fish Marillion is the 1994 release BRAVE. This concept album, with virtually all musical segments joined together to form one long stream-of-consciousness composition, comes the closest to progressive rock and is a favourite of old and new fans alike. The following year's release, AFRAID OF SUNLIGHT, came out at the height of the media frenzy surrounding the OJ Simpson murder trial and lyrically dealt with the pitfalls of our celebrity culture and being caught in the spotlight. Unfortunately, while most of these releases met with critical success, sales continued to fall and Marillion were eventually dropped by EMI.

Their first post-EMI release, THIS STRANGE ENGINE, showed the band making a serious move away from progressive rock. While the title track weighs in at over thirteen minutes and is for all intents and purposes a multi-part composition, the overall feel of the songs has more in common with contemporary or alternative rock than it does with prog. Their latest, RADIATION, is for all intents and purposes a contemporary rock CD.

Musically, like so many of the neo-progressive rock bands, Marillion were a lot harder sounding. There was definitely more of an edge to their music, even their lyrics tended to be more in-your-face when dealing with issues of the day. While they never denied being influenced by Pink Floyd, Yes or even Genesis, they also listed such diverse and equally influential bands as The Doors, Rush, The Beatles and even ABC. Still, many fans cling tenaciously to each Marillion release hoping against hope for a return to their prog roots.

o SCRIPT FOR A JESTERS TEAR (1983 EMI)
o FUGAZI (1984 EMI)
o REAL TO REEL (1984 EMI)
o MISPLACED CHILDHOOD (1985 EMI)
o GARDEN PARTY LIVE EP (1986 EMI)
o CLUTCHING AT STRAWS (1987 EMI)
o THE THIEVING MAGPIE (Live) (1988 EMI)
o SEASONS END (1989 EMI)
o HOLIDAYS IN EDEN (1991 EMI)
o BRAVE (1994 EMI)
o AFRAID OF SUNLIGHT (1995 EMI)
o MADE AGAIN (1996 EMI)
o THIS STRANGE ENGINE (1997 Eaglerock)
o RADIATION (1999 Eaglerock)

# ~ **33** ~
# Moody Blues (England)

The distinction of creating the first, true progressive rock album goes to The
Moody Blues with their release DAYS OF FUTURE PAST in November of 1967. This
LP contained many of progressive rock's trademark elements: longer songs,
changing tempos, Mellotron, use of symphonic orchestra, cosmic lyrics, it's all
there. The album set the tone for what was to come in terms of symphonic
scope and dynamic rock blended into the whole new genre of progressive rock.
The Birmingham based Moody Blues had originally been formed as an R&B group
in 1964 consisting of Mike Pinder (keyboards), Ray Thomas (vocals, flute), Graeme
Edge (drums), Denny Laine (guitar) and Clint Warwick (bass.) They released an
album that year and had significant success with the single *Go Now*.
Unfortunately, the singles that followed didn't do anywhere near as well and
ultimately Laine and Warwick left. They were replaced by Justin Hayward (guitar,
vocals) and John Lodge (bass, vocals), marking the beginning of The Moody Blues
phase two.

In an effort to radically change musical direction the band purchased the new
Mellotron string "sampling" instrument and convinced the record label, Deram,
to let them record with a small symphony. Coinci-dentally, Deram was trying to
show off its new stereo capability and this seemed like the right project to do it
with. Little did they realize the impact that the album would have on future
generations. What made this new musical approach possible was the addition of
Justin Hayward and John Lodge into the Moodies. Their presence cemented the
direction the band would take. DAYS OF FUTURE PAST released in 1967 even left
it's mark on the charts with *Nights in White Satin* and *Tuesday Afternoon*.

The success of that first album led the band to release a series of LP's that
followed along the same mystical musical path. With the purchase of a second
Mellotron to duplicate strings, flutes and choirs, the Moody Blues no longer
needed the full orchestral accompaniment. They became an orchestra on their
own. The albums that followed — IN SEARCH OF THE LOST CHORD, ON THE
THRESHOLD OF A DREAM, TO OUR CHILDREN'S CHILDREN'S CHILDREN, A QUESTION
OF BALANCE, and EVERY GOOD BOY DESERVES FAVOUR from 1968 through to 1971
— all seemed to capture the magical spirit of the times. Each came with a
gatefold sleeve with intricate paintings and illustrations. Each album seemed to
pose the questions to the mysteries of life that teenagers around the world were
asking. And each LP took full advantage of stereo panning, making them required

listening on headphones. And not only that — all of them sold well. It was a time when albums, not singles, began dominating the charts. The Moody Blues launched their own label early in their careers called Threshold. Its first release was TO OUR CHILDREN'S CHILDREN'S CHILDREN. By the time of A QUESTION OF BALANCE, even though the critics had little good to say about them, their fans — the people who actually bought the records — had turned The Moody Blues into one of the rock world's biggest acts.

In 1972 they released SEVENTH SOJOURN containing two of their biggest hit singles: *Isn't Life Strange* and *I'm Just a Singer in a Rock and Roll Band*. The album did well but the musical landscape was changing, breaking into smaller and smaller genres of interest. The Moody Blues were finding their fan base breaking apart. Over the next few years the band didn't record together; instead, each member created solo records. When they came back together in 1977 they released CAUGHT LIVE PLUS FIVE consisting of a live performance from 1969 and leftover unreleased material, the first new group material in years. The double album did well enough to inspire the band to return to the studio and launch phase three of The Moody Blues. In 1978 they released OCTAVE. A new album meant they would have to tour. Mike Pinder declined to go on the road and was replaced by former Yes keyboardist Patrick Moraz. The whirlwind began again with recordings and tours. With Moraz in full time, the band recorded LONG DISTANCE VOYAGER and had a minor hit with *Gemini Dream*. They had an even bigger Top 10 hit with *Your Wildest Dreams* off of the 1986 release THE OTHER SIDE OF LIFE showing that there was still a place for The Moody Blues in the 80's.

In the 90's the band began a series of concerts backed by a full orchestra, something that, strangely, the'y never done before. Playing before capacity crowds of graying baby boomers, and in many cases their children, the response was greater than imagined. The Moody Blues continue to produce their trademark style of music, somewhat mystical and somewhat romantic. Over the years their focus may have changed from the experimentation of the late 60's to the creation of stronger individual songs, but if it weren't for the early efforts of The Moody Blues you might not be reading this book today.

o THE MAGNIFICENT MOODIES (1965 London)
o DAYS OF FUTURE PAST (1967 Deram)
o IN SEARCH OF THE LOST CHORD (1968 Deram)
o ON THE THRESHOLD OF A DREAM (1969 Deram)
o TO OUR CHILDREN'S CHILDREN'S CHILDREN (1969 Threshold)
o A QUESTION OF BALANCE (1970 Threshold)
o EVERY GOOD BOY DESERVES FAVOUR (1971 Threshold)
o SEVENTH SOJOURN (1972 Threshold)
o THIS IS THE MOODY BLUES (Compilation 1974 Threshold)
o IN THE BEGINNING (1975 Deram)
o CAUGHT LIVE PLUS FIVE (1977 Threshold)
o OCTAVE (1978 Threshold)
o OUT OF THIS WORLD (1980 K-Tel Compilation)
o LONG DISTANCE VOYAGER (1981 Threshold)
o THE PRESENT (1983 Threshold)
o VOICES IN THE SKY: BEST OF THE MOODY BLUES (1984 Threshold)
o THE OTHER SIDE OF LIFE (1986 Threshold)
o PRELUDE (1987 Polydor)
o SUR LA MER (1988 Polydor)
o GREATEST HITS (1989 Polydor)
o KEYS TO THE KINGDOM (1991 Polydor)
o THE MOODY BLUES: A NIGHT AT RED ROCKS (1993 Polydor)
o TIME TRAVELLER [BOX SET] (1994 Polygram)

# ~ *34* ~

# The Nice (England)

The Nice are without question one of the premier pioneering progressive rock bands, and one of the first to so heavily use the classics. The prime instigator for this was Keith Emerson, whose keyboard extravaganzas were already getting mammoth headlines well before the birth of Emerson Lake & Palmer.

The Nice got together in early 1967 — starting out as little more than a backing group for P.P. Arnold — playing a mixture of British soul and R&B. Going back even further, Keith Emerson and Lee Jackson played together in an R&B group called Gary Farr & The T-Bones. The Nice came to be Emerson (keyboards), Jackson (bass, vocals), Davy O'List (guitar, vocals) and Brian Davison (drums.) Graduating from a basic backup band to being Arnold's opening act won them high praise and enthusiastic crowd receptions. One of their earliest gigs demonstrated just how determined The Nice were to attract attention to their music: they were performing at the summer 1967 Windsor Rock and Jazz Festival; when it was time for them to go on stage, there were only a few dozen fans milling about; the band set off some smoke bombs; the crowds came running to see what happened; and the Nice exploded into their set. The crowd was speechless, but word of their on-stage theatrics spread throughout the country. Keith Emerson quickly established a reputation not only for his level of musicianship but also his flamboyant keyboard antics. By the fall of 1967 they were on the road with Jimi Hendrix.

At the forefront of the newly arising progressive rock movement, The Nice proved to be adept at pulling elements from non-rock sources and mixing them into a whole new form. From the very beginning it was part of their repertoire to borrow and develop compositions from artists as diverse as Bob Dylan on one end of the spectrum to Leonard Bernstein on the other.

After the release of their first album, THE THOUGHTS OF EMERLIST DAVJACK, guitarist David O'List left the group leaving Emerson and his keyboards to occupy centre stage in the new trio format. Without a guitarist to share the stage, Emerson's theatrics of stabbing the organ and literally throwing it around on stage were totally unhampered. The Nice were instrumental in developing the role that keyboards would play in progressive rock. Over the course of the next two albums, Emerson, who seemed to be more in charge with each passing day, developed his penchant for reworking classical material into a rock format. When

they released ARS LONGA VITA BREVIS, they'd already received significant airplay for their single *America*, even though it clocked in at over six minutes in length. The album added greatly to their already significant fan following. Given that they were playing to packed houses throughout the country, the music press began calling them a supergroup and the publicity machine swung into high gear.

In the fall of 1969 they released THE NICE and it promptly rocketed to the No. 3 position on the charts, where it stayed for some time. Unfortunately for the band, Immediate, their record company, ceased to exist and they were forced to go shopping for another label. They landed at Charisma and there took their musical concept of working with other musical genres, specifically classical, to the next level on FIVE BRIDGES SUITE released in 1970. The album was recorded live at Newcastle City Hall with a full symphony orchestra and it was one of a few albums created at the end of the 60's that attempted to marry rock and classical music to varying degrees of success. Unlike Deep Purple's CONCERTO FOR GROUP AND ORCHESTRA, which suffered from segmenting the rock portion from the classical portion, The Nice worked to create a more natural blending, due in part to Emerson's classical piano style of playing and composing. There's no question that FIVE BRIDGES SUITE helped lay the corner-stone for future symphonic prog rock efforts. Still, all was not well with The Nice. By this time Emerson was putting ELP together and consequently his heart was no longer in the band. Their last recording, ELEGY, was more of a contractual fulfillment than anything else. On the plus side, both of these albums were wonderfully ambitious for the times and certainly harbingers of things to come for ELP and progressive rock in general.

The Nice were packing halls throughout England and Europe and yet, just as they were on the verge of capitalizing on their popularity in the states, they broke up. Both Jackson and Davidson were getting tired of seemingly secondary roles to Emerson's ever increasing showmanship and all parties agreed to go their separate ways. Emerson, as we all know, went on to create ELP, while Jackson and Davidson eventually joined up with newcomer Patrick Moraz to form Refugee.

- THE THOUGHTS OF EMERLIST DAVJACK (1967 Immediate)
- ARS LONGA VITA BREVIS (1969 Immediate)
- THE NICE (1969 Immediate)
- FIVE BRIDGES SUITE (1970 Charisma)
- KEITH EMERSON WITH THE NICE (1971 Polygram)
- ELEGY (1971 Charisma)
- NICE — THE IMMEDIATE STORY (1975 Sire)
- THE NICE COLLECTION (1985 Castle)
- THE IMMEDIATE YEARS (1995 Charly)
- THE BEST OF THE NICE (1995 Griffin Music)
- BBC SESSION: AMERICA (1996 Receiver)
- THE BEST OF THE NICE (1998 Essential)

# ~ 35 ~
# Oldfield, Mike (England)

When it came to pushing the studio to new heights, Reading born Mike Oldfield made history with his first release entitled TUBULAR BELLS. Oldfield was just a teenager when he started performing folk music with his sister. They released one album entitled SALLYANGIE in 1968. After putting his own band together to no success, he joined up with Kevin Ayers And The Whole World playing both bass and guitar until they fell apart in 1971. During this time he'd been working on an ambitious fifty minute demo tape, but was finding no record company interest. It wasn't until he crossed paths with Richard Branson that things came together. Branson was at the time owner of the highly successful chain of Virgin record stores. But he aspired to more. After hearing Oldfield's demo tape, he saw the perfect vehicle to launch his own record label. Branson arranged for Oldfield to spend all the time he needed in the studio, overdubbing each and every instrument to complete his epic composition. In May of 1973 TUBULAR BELLS became the first release for Branson's new label, Virgin Records. The critics were very kind and the LP sold well. TUBULAR BELLS became a massive hit. In the United States sales were helped when portions of the composition was used in the movie The Exorcist.

The media quickly dubbed Oldfield "the man of a 1000 overdubs" and true to form he was back in the studio working on his next epic which turned out to be HERGEST RIDGE in 1974. It rocketed up the charts and for a time HERGEST RIDGE occupied the No. 1 slot, while TUBULAR BELLS stubbornly clung to No. 2. As if that wasn't enough, the following year he released OMMADAWN, which again did extremely well on the album charts. All three of these records Oldfield composed as complete works, separated only by the need to flip the disc over.

Over the next few years, Oldfield took a break from composing new material and concentrated on presenting TUBULAR BELLS with a full orchestra and working with Virgin records to create a boxed-set of his early work. Always shy about working live, he did manage to tour Europe which resulted in a double LP live disc entitled EXPOSED. In 1979 he recorded PLATINUM (or AIRBORNE as it was called in America.) Having accomplished all he that could playing virtually all the instruments himself, Oldfield moved away from the long instrumental compositions. He began working with selected vocalists and other musicians to craft songs of varying lengths. The 1980 release QE2 expanded on Oldfield's shorter compositions and featured Genesis producer David Hentschel (keyboards), Maggie Riley (vocals), Phil Collins and Morris Pert (drums.) Much like Alan Parson's, Oldfield formed a loose collection of talented individuals to work with on future projects. With this arrangement he created FIVE MILES OUT and CRISES.

For the 1984 release DISCOVERY, Oldfield returned to handling most of the playing himself, with vocal assistance once again from Maggie Rielly and Barry Palmer and Simon Phillips on drums. The albums released during this period tended to be made up mostly of shorter four minute songs with a token long ten or twelve minute track, which hardly made use of his skills. That same year he composed a soundtrack for the film THE KILLING FIELDS.

After a brief layoff, Oldfield came back with ISLANDS, working once again with Simon Phillips and featuring guest appearances by Bonnie Tyler and old friend Kevin Ayers. Tyler was riding high in the charts and her inclusion was no doubt

an effort to get Oldfield back on the singles charts, however nothing came of it. Other than for his solid base of fans, Oldfield had become very unfashionable.

Oldfield went on to write and record many more fine examples of progressive rock, while Virgin Records became one of the most successful and respected progressive rock labels. Toward the end of the 80's, Oldfield became unhappy with the terms of his original Virgin agreement and he made his displeasure known to Virgin boss Richard Branson. The conflict came to an end with the final Virgin release in 1991, HEAVEN'S OPEN. This recording contains a couple compositions which take aim at Virgin's apparent overriding concern for commercial success at the cost of originality and musicianship. Oldfield left the label and later still the label was sold to one of the giant conglomerates.

Far from having given up, Oldfield continued to record and, in 1996, released the Celtic inspired VOYAGER, featuring a strong influence of the traditional and contemporary. In 1998, to mark the 25th anniversary of his first musical creation, he re-visited tried and true territory with TUBULAR BELLS III, a major reworking of many of the original themes, some that seemed to reflect a very danceable feel. Unlike the lackluster response to the earlier TUBULAR BELLS II, this release received a positive nod from critics in all corners.

 o TUBULAR BELLS (1973 Virgin)
 o HERGEST RIDGE (1974 Virgin)

*Oldfield, Mike*

o THE ORCHESTRAL TUBULAR BELLS (1975 Virgin)
o OMMADAWN (1975 Virgin)
o BOXED (1976 Virgin)
o INCANTATIONS (1978 Virgin)
o EXPOSED (1979 Virgin)
o QE2 (1980 Virgin)
o PLATINUM (1980 Virgin)
o IMPRESSIONS (1979 Virgin Compilation)
o AIRBORNE (1980 Virgin Compilation)
o MUSIC WONDERLAND (1980 Virgin)
o FIVE MILES OUT (1982 Virgin)
o CRISES (1983 Virgin)
o DISCOVERY (1984 Virgin)
o THE KILLING FIELD [SOUNDTRACK] (1984 Virgin)
o THE COMPLETE MIKE OLDFIELD (1987 Virgin)
o ISLANDS (1987 Virgin)
o A VIRGIN COMPILATION (1987 Virgin)
o EARTHMOVING (1989 Virgin)
o AMAROK (90 Virgin)
o COLLECTORS EDITION BOX I (1990 Virgin)
o COLLECTORS EDITION BOX II (1990 Virgin)
o HEAVEN'S OPEN (1991 Virgin)
o TUBULAR BELLS II (1992 Virgin)
o ELEMENTS (1993 Virgin Box)
o THE BEST OF ELEMENTS (1993 Virgin)
o THE SONGS OF DISTANT EARTH (1995)
o VOYAGER (1996 WEA)
o XXV THE ESSENTIAL (1997 WEA)
o TUBULAR BELLS III (1998 WEA)

# ~ 36 ~
# Omega (Hungary)

Omega was one of the first bands from behind the Iron Curtain to break onto
the progressive music scene. They were without question one of Hungary's most
popular rock bands, and to fans of the genre they pointed to a world of music
heretofore not explored. There was a rumour going around in the early days of
prog that bands like Omega were able to create progressive rock music in a

society that shunned western rock only because prog contained more musical depth and was, of course, closely aligned to the classics. Whether or not there was ever anything to that rumour, it sure seemed that most of the popular rock bands out of the East seemed to prefer progressive rock.

Omega was formed over 30 years ago in early 1968 and interestingly have maintained a very stable lineup. Other than a few personnel changes early in their career, their lineup has consisted of Janos Kobor (lead vocals), Laszlo Benko (keyboards), Gyorgy Molnar (guitars), Tamas Mihaly (bass) and Ferenc Debreceni (drums.) Given their tenure, Omega has had a chance to create many different musical styles. They've been described as essentially a hard rock band with prog tendencies and, to some degree, that's true. Their recordings have all the prog prerequisites including some wonderful guitar and keyboard interplay. Over the years their recordings have been done in both their native language and English. Their earlier Hungarian recordings tend to sound a little rough at the edges, but by the time they were signed to the German Bellaphon label the group had made great strides musically, not to mention having access to better studios.

By 1975 the band had hit its stride during what some refer to as the "golden age" of progressive rock. They traveled to England and recorded HALL OF FLOATERS IN THE SKY, which also featured some well arranged orchestral accompaniment. This led to the 1976 release TIME ROBBER which can best be described as a blending of Pink Floyd and Eloy influences. Never moving out of cult status outside of their native land, the band continued to record material well into the 90's. It's only by looking back over their cumulative efforts that you get a sense of their influence. Few bands can boast of over 25 recordings, with combined sales of many millions. And to drive home the point, even into the early 90's Omega was drawing huge audiences and even getting national TV exposure for their efforts.

Their history can be divided into three periods: their first few LP's up to the early 70's were heavily influenced with a psychedelic flavour; the recordings through the 70's and into the early 80's took on a more progressive rock influence; and for the later 80's releases their music became more influenced by Tangerine Dream with synths, sequencers and computers. Following their discography is a little tricky given that Omega released a series of both Hungarian and English recordings. The English recordings, released mostly on the German Bellaphon or Decca labels, tended to feature many of the Hungarian pieces re-recorded and rearranged in a more accomplished manner. It should be noted that at the time of this writing Omega was selling tickets for yet another concert in Hungary. Alive and kicking after thirty years.

- TROMBITAS FREDI (1968 Qualiton)
- OMEGA RED STAR FROM HUNGARY (1968 Qualiton)*
- 10,000 LEPES (1969 Qualiton)
- EJSZAKAI ORSZAGUT (1970 Pepita)
- ELO LIVE (1972 Pepita)
- OMEGA (1973 Bellaphon)*
- 200 YEARS AFTER THE LAST WAR (1974 Bellaphon)*
- OMEGA III (1974 Bellaphon)*
- THE HALL OF THE FLOATERS IN THE SKY (1975 Bellaphon)*
- NEM TUDOM A NEVED (1976 Pepita)
- TIME ROBBERS (1976 Decca)*
- IDORABLO (1977 Pepita)
- ON TOUR (1977 Bellaphon)
- CSILLAGOK UTJAN (1978 Pepita)
- SKYROVER (1978 Bellaphon)*
- GAMMAPOLIS (1979 Bellaphon)*
- LIVE AT THE KISSTADION '79 (1979 Pepita)
- ARRANYALBUM 1969-1971 (1979 WEA)
- KISSTADION 80 (1980 WEA)

o AZ ARC (1981)
o WORKING (1981 WEA)*
o OMEGA XI (1982 Barclay)
o JUBILLEUM KONCERT (1983 Barclay)
o LEGENDAS KISLEMEZEK 1967-1971 (1984 Barclay)
o A FOLD ARNYEKOS OLDALAN (1986 Barclay)
o BABYLON (1987)
o OMEGA 1968-1973 (1992)
o AZ OMEGA OSSZES KISLEMEZE (1992)
o EGI VANDOR: OMEGA 1974-1981 (1993)
o NEPSTADION (1994)
o TRANS AND DANCE (1995)
o NEPSTADION KONCERT 1994 NO. 1 (1995)
o NEPSTADION KONCERT NO. 2 (1995)
o AS OMEGA OSSZES KONCERTFELVETELE (1995)
* indicates English releases

# ~ **37** ~

# PFM (Italy)

As one third of Italian "big three", PFM — or Premiata Forneria Marconi — are one of the most celebrated Italian progressive rock bands. Each of the members spent their formative years touring with a variety of cover bands honing their musicianship. When it all came together with the formation of PFM they took their inspiration from Genesis, Jethro Tull, ELP, King Crimson and Yes, but went on to create a musical style that was uniquely their own.

The members of PFM had been playing in various Italian beat bands during the mid- to late-60's. One of them, Quelli, became quite successful doing cover tunes from groups like The Turtles and even Traffic. Towards the end of 1970, after some internal friction, four members — Quelli, Franz Di Cioccio, Franco Mussida, Flavio Premoli and Giorgio Piazza — formed PFM, taking their name from a pastry shop in a town near Milan. In 1971, they added multi-instrumentalist Mauro Pagani on violin. It was his appearance that provided the creative spark and brought all of the progressive rock elements together.

By early 1971 they were on the road supporting bands like Yes and Procol Harum. As always, the road work prepared their musicianship for the writing and recording that was to come. The first LP, STORIA DI UNO MINUTO, which in English

means History of a Minute, was released in January of 1972, while the second, PER UN AMICO, was released in November of the same year. PFM was already on its way to international recognition.

In 1974, PFM toured the United States for four months and headlined with a variety of bands including The Kinks and Poco at the famed Fillmore East. PFM was on the verge of breaking into the large U.S. market when things started to unravel. Two elements impacted the future of PFM: homesickness and politics. Never having been this far from home for so long, along with the stressful lifestyle of performing and traveling night after night, caused the band to cut short their time in the U.S. and return home. Their decision was aided by the response, or lack of response, that they were getting from the American record executives as a result of PFM's concerts performed for PLO sympathizers.

Unknown to many fans who are only familiar with the English versions of the songs, was PFM's heavily politicized Italian lyrics. Englishman Pete Sinfield had been hired to write the English lyrics for the first two PFM LP's. For his first album with the band he chose not to actually translate the Italian lyrics, but instead came up with completely new material and set it to the existing music. For the second English release, WORLD BECAME THE WORLD, Sinfield was asked to create more of literal translation of the Italian lyrics. He completed the task, but not sharing their political leanings, Sinfield chose not to work with the band in the future.

Following their return to Italy, Piazza left to concentrate on production work and was replaced by a Frenchman from Nice, Patrick Dijvas. In 1976 Pagani left to work as a solo artist, and over the next five years there were many personnel changes. With the release of JET LAG in 1977 the band adopted more of a jazz or fusion influence in their compositions. In 1980 PFM recorded an album called SUONARE SUONARE which focused on the American Dream. After this release Premoli left the group. He was replaced by Lucio Fabbri on keyboards and violin.

PFM continued to tour and record through the 80's, but like so many others, they moved further from their progressive rock roots and more into a mainstream pop sound. At last report the band continues to exist and tour.

o STORIA DI UN MINUTO (1971 Numero Uno)
o PER UN AMICO (1972 Numero Uno)
o PHOTO'S OF GHOSTS (1973 Manticore)
o THE WORLD BECAME THE WORLD (1974 Manitcore)
o LIVE IN THE USA (1974 Numero Uno)
o CHOCOLATE KINGS (1976 Numero Uno)
o JET LAG (1977 Numero Uno)
o PASSPARTU (1978 Numero Uno)
o SUONARE SUONARE (1980 Numero Uno)
o COMETI VA IN RIVA ALLA CITTA (1981 Numero Uno)
o IMPRESSIONI VENT'ANNI DOPO (1994)
o BOBO CLUB 2000 - 1972 (1994)
o 10 ANNI LIVE 1971 -1981 (1996 RTI Music)

# ~ 38 ~

# Pink Floyd (England)

Formed in 1965, Pink Floyd was Rick Wright (keyboards), Roger Waters (bass), Nick Mason (drums) and Syd Barrett (guitar.) They took their name from two Georgia bluesmen: Pink Anderson and Floyd Council. By early 1966 they were the underground's "official" band and could be seen and heard regularly at the Marquee Club's Sunday afternoon "Spontaneous Underground" affairs. Their first mainstream attention came when they headlined an all night benefit party for the underground paper *The International Times* in October 1966. This was quickly and strategically followed by benefit concerts for other important causes including one for Oxfam where they performed at the prestigious Royal Albert Hall. On top of all this they became the house band for the new underground club UFO.

In 1967, as the Beatles were working on SGT. PEPPER at Abby Road studios. And just down the hall Pink Floyd was working on their first LP. Released in August during the so-called "summer of love", the album features Syd Barrett at his psychedelic best. The album PIPER AT THE GATES OF DAWN was received well, and Pink Floyd was whisked away for a brief tour of America. But by this time Syd was deeply involved with psychedelic drugs. It got to the point where he would appear on talk shows and not respond to questions, or show up on stage and strum one chord the whole night. When they returned to England the band called up a friend, Dave Gilmore, to help out. For a time Gilmore even appeared on stage with Barrett. Then one day the band was off to a gig and didn't bother to pick Syd up. The second album, A SAUCERFUL OF SECRETS, was released in 1968 on the same day as the band performed in London's Hyde Park along with Roy Harper and Jethro Tull. The second release began to show some spacey influences, particularly in compositions such as *Set the Controls for the Heart of the Sun*. The album contained a number of holdover tracks from Barrett, but also displayed Roger Waters' increasing control over the band's material. With the release of UMMAGUMMA in 1969 Pink Floyd was firmly established not only as a progressive rock band but they were also at the forefront of a new genre called space-rock. With their long droning organ and spacey guitar sounds the band created music that many got high to. They developed their compositional and musical skills throughout this period, which culminated in 1973 with the landmark DARK SIDE OF THE MOON. The band spent nine months in the studio working with the as yet virtually unknown producer Alan Parsons to create an audio masterpiece that holds up to this day. The album eventually spent over 700 weeks on the charts and, much as the Beatles had achieved with SGT. PEPPER,

became a milestone recording in the world of rock music.

The critics, not wanting to feel too much a part of the crowd, tended to like the band's follow-up in 1975, WISH YOU WERE HERE, a little more, dealing as it did with the loss of genius and it's veiled references to the fading brilliance of Syd Barrett.

By 1977 and the release of ANIMALS, Roger Waters had more or less taken charge of Pink Floyd's lyrical vision. He used this and the next two albums to exorcise a variety of demons pent up within his soul. Pink Floyd was big news, with every release doing well on the charts and the tours selling out. It all got a bit too much for Waters who used the double record set THE WALL in 1979 to lambaste the arena-rock spectaculars Pink Floyd had in many ways helped create. The album produced a huge hit with *Another Brick In The Wall Part 2*. By the time of THE FINAL CUT in 1983, Waters was in charge of everything and the rest of the band were virtually session players. Something had to give, and Pink Floyd ended in a messy divorce. The members all headed off to work on various solo projects, the most successful of which belonged strangely enough to Waters.

After five years Gilmore got together with Wright and Mason to record a new Pink Floyd record. Word of this leaked to Waters, who felt that without his involvement they really couldn't be called Pink Floyd. A flurry of lawsuits resulted and in the end the rest of the band won the right to carry on using the name. They produced A MOMENTARY LAPSE OF REASON which, for the most part, picked up on Pink Floyd circa 1975 before Water's dominance. The band toured to sell-out spectaculars around the world and in 1994 released THE DIVISION BELL, once again displaying Pink Floyd at their collective creative best, with virtually all composition being shared by Gilmore, Wright and Mason. Yet another monstrous tour and live CD followed bringing us up date.

Pink Floyd continue to be a force within not only the progressive rock genre but the mainstream rock community. Regardless of what the critics have tried to say over the years, the efforts of Pink Floyd, if anything, demonstrate the public's willingness to listen to and appreciate, if given the opportunity, what prog has to offer. In many respects Pink Floyd, with their musical experimentation and obsessive search for studio perfection, changed the way we listened to music.

- o PIPER AT THE GATES OF DAWN (1967 Capitol)
- o A SAUCERFUL OF SECRETS (1968 Capitol)
- o MORE (1969 Capitol)
- o UMMAGUMMA (1969 Harvest)
- o ATOM HEART MOTHER (1970 Harvest)
- o MEDDLE (1971 Harvest)
- o RELICS (1971 Harvest)
- o OBSCURED BY CLOUDS (1972 Harvest)
- o NICE PAIR (1973 Capitol)
- o DARK SIDE OF THE MOON (1973 Harvest)
- o WISH YOU WERE HERE (1975 Columbia)
- o ANIMALS (1977 Columbia)
- o THE WALL (1979 Columbia)

o COLLECTION OF GREAN DANCE SONGS (1981 Columbia)
o THE FINAL CUT (1983 Columbia)
o WORKS (1983 Capitol)
o MOMENTARY LAPSE OF REASON (1987 Columbia)
o DELICATE SOUND OF THUNDER (1988 Columbia)
o SHINE ON BOX SET (1992 Columbia)
o THE DIVISION BELL (1994 Columbia)
o PULSE (1995 Columbia)

# ~ 39 ~
# Procol Harum (England)

The roots of Procol Harum begin in the early 60's with a group called The Paramounts consisting of Gary Brooker (keyboards), Chris Copping (bass), B.J. Wilson (drums) and Robin Trower (guitar.) The Paramounts were a basic R&B group, but Brooker aspired to something greater and was writing more adventurous material on the side. Choosing to leave The Paramounts, Brooker joined up with Keith Reid to add lyrics to his music. At the same time he took out an add in the music papers and finally created Procol Harum apparently named after Reid's cat, consisting of himself, Reid, Bobby Harrison (drums), Ray Rowyer (guitar), Mathew Fisher (keyboards) and David Knights (bass.) This was the lineup responsible for Procol Harum's first single, a number one hit, *A Whiter Shade of Pale* and a self-titled album.

Internal friction over credits left the band without a guitarist or drummer. Undaunted, Brooker called upon Trower and Wilson from the Paramounts to join. Thus constituted they returned to the studio. Having had little luck with a follow-up single, they concentrated on recording a more experimental album and thus was born SHINE ON BRIGHTLY in 1968. It contained the band's first prog epic, the 18 minute *In Held Twas In I*, a multi-sectional symphonic prog composition featuring a plethora of influences and an overriding plaintive tone due in part to Brooker's unique vocal style.

In 1969 they followed up with A SALTY DOG. No epics this time, just ten compositions featuring a blend of the classics, lush orchestration, sound effects, a hint of their original R&B roots and the amazing story telling from the pen of Keith Reid. The title track became a signature tune for the band overnight. The album did better in America than Britain, where the band was still regarded as a

one-hit wonder. Following this release both Fisher and Knights left to be replaced by another ex Paramount-er Chris Copping. The foursome, with Reid on the side for lyrics but fully credited on the albums, then recorded HOME in 1970 and BROKEN BARRICADES in 1971. Here the material featured a more aggressive guitar sound, with compositions at times stretching to over seven minutes, but mostly in the five-plus range, which was still considered quite long for the time. But it still wasn't enough for Trower who left to form his own group. The band then recruited Dave Ball (guitar) and Alan Cartwright (bass.) In late 1971 Procol Harum traveled to Canada to perform with the Edmonton Symphony Orchestra. The resulting live album was hugely successful and sold millions producing a top 20 hit with *Conquistador*. Even the critics hailed it a masterpiece. It all took the band by surprise. They postponed plans to record a new studio album and quickly arranged a massive North American tour to take advantage of their sudden popularity.

It was 1973 by the time they completed their next studio offering, GRAND HOTEL, on which Dave Ball was replaced by Mick Grabham (guitar.) They also produced EXOTIC BIRDS AND FRUIT in 1974 with the same lineup. In an attempt to inject some external success for the 1975 release PROCOL'S NINTH, the band worked with noted pop producers Jerry Leiber and Mike Stoller, even going so far as to record one of their songs. Typically, no single made any impact on the charts.

After a two year break Procol Harum returned to the recording scene. By this time Alan Cartwright had left, so Chris Copping moved back onto bass and newcomer Pete Solley took up the keyboards. Their final album of the 70's proved to be an attempt at former glories and was perhaps their best to date, successfully blending all of the elements which made Procol Harum unique. SOMETHING MAGIC contained wonderful shorter songs like the title track, the classically oriented *Skating on Thin Ice*, the starkly aggressive and mysterious *Mark of the Claw*, and even another 18 minute epic, *The Worm and the Tree*. Unfortunately it was not a sign of things to come.

It had been ten years since Procol Harum had come on the music scene and they decided to call it a day. Gary Brooker went off on a solo career while other members took off to other ventures. After three albums of interesting solo material Gary Brooker and Mathew Fisher got together and explored the possibility of creating another Procol Harum album. They enlisted Robin Trower once again and a number of session players and produced the 1991 PRODIGAL STRANGER with Keith Reid, as always, handling the words. While a fine release when compared with Brooker's solo efforts, it failed to live up to expectations and and the glories of the past.

The music of Procol Harum, even the rockier pieces, tended to have an air of the classics to it. The music was always dramatic, dynamic and very much larger than life. Even in many of the shorter tracks there is suspense created, in large part, by the wonderful lyrics crafted by Reid. His choice of subject matter, whether it be the swashbuckling salty seas of *A Salty Dog*, the comic tale of a sexually transmitted disease in *Souvenir of London* or the philosophical epics of the Worm, managed to successfully capture the many moods of progressive rock.

o PROCOL HARUM (1967 Deram)
o SHINE ON BRIGHTLY (1968 A&M)
o A SALTY DOG (1969 A&M)
o HOME (1970 A&M)
o BROKEN BARRICADES (1971 A&M)
o LIVE IN CONCERT WITH THE EDMONTON SYMPHONY ORCHESTRA (1972 A&M)
o THE BEST OF PROCOL HARUM (1973 A&M)
o GRAND HOTEL (1973 Chrysalis)
o EXOTIC BIRDS AND FRUIT (1974 Chrysalis)
o PROCOL'S NINTH (1975 Chrysalis)
o SOMETHING MAGIC (1977 Chrysalis)
o CLASSICS, VOL. 17 (1987 A&M)
o PRODIGAL STRANGER (1991 Zoo)

# ~ **40** ~

# Renaissance (England)

One of the bands that epitomized progressive rock's blending of musical styles, yet managed to create music that retained each style's distinctiveness was Renaissance. They incorporated classical musical motifs into longer compositions that spoke about larger than life tales. Just as importantly, they were one of the first prog bands to feature a female vocalist, which in itself created a completely original melodic style for their compositions. The first incarnation of this band was created by ex-Yardbirds guitarist Keith Relf and drummer Jim McCarty. They recruited Relf's sister Jane (vocals), ex-Nashville Teens John Hawken (keyboards) and Louis Cennamo (bass.) Relf and McCarty were not keen on the louder style of Yardbirds then being pursued by new guitarist Jimmy Page. Instead, they chose to go in the other direction. The music they created in Renaissance was an astonishing departure from the music of the Yardbirds. They relied less on their R&B past, and incorporated those other musical influences such as classical, folk and even psychedelic in a 1969 release simply called RENAISSANCE. It was groundbreaking at the time and Jane Relf's softer vocals made the music standout that much more.

The LP was well received in the U.S. and a tour ensued. Unfortunately the band was booked on a blues circuit and crowd response was less than enthusiastic for the new material. Group moral plummeted and McCarty was reminded of how incessant touring had fueled his desire to leave the Yardbirds. A tour of Europe was canceled and the members retreated to the seclusion of working on a new recording. Relf and McCarty decided to cease being performing members. Hawken called upon old pals Terry Crowe (vocals) and Michael Dunford (guitar) and recruited Terry Slade (drums) to fill the slots. A second LP, entitled ILLUSION, was recorded following in the style of the first. The record company, seeing the success of louder bands such as Led Zeppelin, felt it was inferior and lacked the energy to compete in the shops. Consequently they let it sit on the shelf for several months and fan response was weak when it eventually was released. Relf and McCarty were unhappy with the overall experience and left the group in 1971, leaving the rest of the band to form around Dunford, Jon Camp (bass), Terry Sullivan (drums) and John Tout (keyboards.) The addition of Annie Haslim, a singer with operatic background and a three-octave range, established Renaissance as one of progressive rock's most melodic and ambitious acts.

The first couple albums, PROLOGUE (1972) and ASHES ARE BURNING (1973),

showed this second incarnation of the band as even more adventurous than the first in terms of musical style, composition and arranging. The classical influences are more overt in this version of Renaissance, particularly Nineteenth century composers like Chopin. The success of the first two releases spurred the band on to even greater heights. Their compositions became more self-assured, the arranging became fuller and the production became cleaner. The band, for the

*Renaissance*

most part, relocated to America for a couple of years to focus on a small but growing fan base, particularly on the East Coast where they played live regularly. 1974's TURN OF THE CARDS contains the classic track most representative of this period, *Mother Russia*, while the 1975 release SCHEHERAZADE & OTHER SHORT STORIES contains the twenty five minute epic *Songs of Scheherazade*. The band continued to produce a steady stream of top quality progressive rock releases, however their audience failed to grow substantially and Renaissance never cracked the musical mainstream. Additionally, their music was clashing with the punk rock and new wave of the day. It was clear by the 1978 release A SONG FOR ALL SEASONS that the material was falling on deaf ears at the record company level as the focus shifted to the latest musical fad-de-jour.

Renaissance continued to record and release through to the mid-80's, but with their later LP's they attempted to move more into the mainstream of music and further away from their prog roots. By 1983's TIME LINE, it was down to four to five minute streamlined compositions, steady beats and all geared to getting radio airplay. Still regarded by radio programmers as part of the prog scene of the 70's, the album was ignored and the members decided to call it a day, going their separate ways, some heading back to England to work in other groups or sessions and some to stay in America doing solo work.

One of the many ways that Renaissance left their mark in the world of prog was that of having a female vocalist up front. Both Jane Relf and then Annie Haslam set the tone for female vocalists in the progressive rock genre. In the 90's Renaissance returned with two different groupings, one with Annie Haslam and the other led by Michael Dunford. Each released recordings under the Renaissance banner, but neither fully captured the magic of the original. As of this writing there were rumours that the original band was attempting to reform and record yet again.

- o RENAISSANCE (1969 Warner Bros.)
- o ILLUSION (1970 Warner Bros.)
- o PROLOG (1972 Capitol)
- o ASHES ARE BURNING (1973 Capitol)
- o TURN OF THE CARDS (1974 Sire)
- o SCHEHERAZADE (1975 Sire)
- o LIVE AT CARNEGIE HALL (1976 Sire)
- o NOVELLA (1977 Sire)
- o A SONG FOR ALL SEASONS (1978 Warner Bros.)
- o IN THE BEGINNING (1978 Capitol Repackage)
- o AZURE D'OR (1979 Warner Bros.)
- o ROCK GALAXY (1980 RCA Compilation)
- o CAMERA CAMERA (1981 IRS)

o TIME LINE (1983 IRS)
o TALES OF 1001 NIGHTS,VOL. I (1990 Sire Compilation)
o TALES OF 1001 NIGHTS VOL. 2 (1990 Sire Compilation)
o BLESSING IN DISGUISE [WITH HASLAM] (1996)
o THE OTHER WOMAN [WITH DUNFORD] (1996 HTD)

# ~ 41 ~
# Rush (Canada)

Canada's Rush started out as a straight ahead hard rock band forming in 1969 and then releasing their first self-titled LP in 1974. As a three piece their inspiration came from bands like Cream and even Led Zeppelin. A change in personnel for the second LP, FLY BY NIGHT, brought in lyricist and drummer Neil Peart, he along with bassist Geddy Lee and guitarist Alex Lifeson were about to become legendary.

While their first album contained a couple of songs over the seven minute range, their style of composition had a long way to go. The early stuff was straight ahead power trio rock. However, with the addition of Peart for the second album, the band's compositional style and arranging started to take on new dimensions with material like *By-Tor and the Snow Dog*. Perhaps just as important, their re-mix engineer from the first album, Terry Brown, became their producer, a relationship that would last for many years.

Their third release, CARESS OF STEEL in 1975, contained their first concept piece, the side-long *Fountain of Lamneth*. Unfortunately the album was completely passed over by almost everyone. All of the elements were there, but the band had yet to find that successful spark. So once again under the direction of Terry Brown, Rush returned to the studio in 1976 to record 2112 with it's side-long sci-fi oriented title track. Conceptually and lyrically it was true-blue progressive rock, with the individual triumphing over an impersonal and technologically bound society. This LP, more than CARESS OF STEEL, exposed Rush to a prog audience. For the next two albums Rush continued to develop the sci-fi themes. A FAREWELL TO KINGS in 1977 also contained the FM radio hit *Closer to the Heart* which became a concert staple for many years, and HEMISPHERES in 1978 featured its eighteen minute epic title song. By this time Rush had found their stride, creating longer compositions with a mixture of acoustic and electric guitar, complicated bass and drum lines and a hint of keyboards. Compositionally the

copyright 1981 Phil Anderson / KAOS2000 Magazine

albums all contained longer pieces with many musical twists and turns.

After a series of tours and a break from recording the band released PERMANENT WAVES in 1980. The album contained another concert and airplay staple in the form of *Spirit of Radio*. With this release the band began one of it's many stylistic changes. The songs were getting less fantasy oriented as Peart's writing style matured and they were moving ever so slightly away from a prog style. The overt prog period for Rush culminated with MOVING PICTURES. This album featured more keyboards than ever before in songs such as *Tom Sawyer* and *Limelight*. Many prog fans list this as their favourite release. As if to signal the end of each era, Rush began releasing multiple-disc live albums from their most recent tours. Such was the case here with 1981's EXIT STAGE LEFT.

Through the 80's Rush streamlined their compositional style, but still released material of great maturity for a loud rock band. Long-time producer Terry Brown bid farewell after his last project, 1982's SIGNALS. Neal Peart's lyrics grew in intensity as he tackled more and more topical issues with each album's almost concept-like proportions, such as 1985's POWER WINDOWS, where each song deals with some aspect of cultural power. Rush's next recording, under the production of Peter Collins, HOLD YOUR FIRE in 1987, again showed a slight change in developmental style as the band's material became very produced. This changed again for the 1989's PRESTO where the band returned to a more stripped-down open sound, this time with Rupert Hine handling the production. Hine returned for 1991's ROLL THE BONES which continued the bare and basic sound. Two years later Peter Collins returned and the band released COUNTERPARTS which was a continuation of their more guitar oriented style, and it continued in a similar fashion for the 1996 release TEST FOR ECHO.

Something should be said for the packaging of Rush recordings because, like many progressive rock bands, the album packaging said a lot about what was inside. Many of their records were delivered in fold-out packages designed by Hugh Syme whose association with the band started with CARESS OF STEEL and continues to TEST FOR ECHO. The artwork and graphics were all connected to each album's particular theme and were always full of visual subtleties. Rush have never been short of words and that carried through in their album credits where they paid particular attention to the smallest detail and gave credit to all members of their team.

While Rush continued to produce AOR material of the highest quality through the 80's and into the 90's very little of it would actually qualify as progressive rock. The band members over the years in many interviews have been asked about the changing musical direction and, while not disowning the prog tag, made it clear that as a musical unit they needed to change. Yet there are many in their prog fan base who remain hopeful that Rush might someday return to those progressive rock roots.

- o RUSH (1974 Anthem)
- o FLY BY NIGHT (1975 Anthem)
- o CARESS OF STEEL (1975 Anthem)
- o 2112 (1976 Anthem)
- o ALL THE WORLD'S A STAGE (1977 Anthem)
- o A FAREWELL TO KINGS (1977 Anthem)
- o HEMISPHERES (1978 Anthem)
- o PERMANENT WAVES (1980 Anthem)
- o MOVING PICTURES (1981 Anthem)
- o EXIT STAGE LEFT (1981 Anthem)
- o SIGNALS (1982 Anthem)
- o GRACE UNDER PRESSURE (1984 Anthem)
- o POWER WINDOWS (1985 Anthem)

- o HOLD YOUR FIRE (1987 Anthem)
- o PRESTO (1989 Anthem)
- o A SHOW OF HANDS (1989 Anthem)
- o ROLL THE BONES (1991 Anthem)
- o CHRONICLES (1991 Anthem Compilation)
- o COUNTERPARTS (1993 Anthem)
- o TEST FOR ECHO (1996 Anthem)
- o DIFFERENT STAGES (1999 Anthem)

# ~ 42 ~

# Soft Machine (England)

Taking their name from the William Burrough's novel, The Soft Machine had been together since August 1966, around the time of the third version of The Wilde Flowers, that influential band who were the springboard for the Canterbury sound. The Soft's lineup was forever changing and eventually saw over 15 different permutations. They established themselves on the London underground scene playing at the usual venues like UFO and The Roundhouse. They also performed with Pink Floyd at The 14 Hour Technicolor Dream in 1967 and made quite an impact.

In the beginning The Soft Machine was Robert Wyatt (drums), Mike Ratledge (keyboards), Kevin Ayers (bass, vocals) and Daevid Allen (guitar.) Their first single was released in mid-1967 and featured rhythm guitar by Jimi Hendrix who was in the studio recording his own *Hey Joe*" single. However, the Soft's release had no impact on the charts so the band took off to perform some concerts in France. When they tried to return, all of the members were allowed back except Daevid Allen. Immigration listed him as an "undesirable". He stayed in France and formed Gong shortly thereafter. Their earlier association with Hendrix resulted in a three-month support tour in America in early 1968. While in New York the band, now a trio, recorded their first self-titled album over four days. Unlike their later work, The Soft Machine's first recordings were influenced by psychedelia and featured many shorter pop style pieces, similar to Syd Barrett era Pink Floyd. Both of these events, the tour and recording, proved quite stressful and the band actually broke up. It wasn't until 1969 when the record was about to be released in America that Robert Wyatt was asked to reform the band. With a new lineup that included Wyatt, Ratledge, Hugh Hopper (bass) plus horn players, they recorded VOLUME TWO, then took off on another tour. Many consider this period

as the band's finest and most creative phase. Unfortunately the same lineup would never record together again.

The vocals were phased out by the third album and the band was left to create music based around the organ work of Mike Ratledge. The music at this point lost much of its early psychedelic flavour as the band began creating longer jazz influenced compositions. From this point The Soft Machine released an album a year, THIRD in 1970 through SEVEN in 1974. Each album was with a slightly different lineup and each focused on a more fusion-jazz sound. Typically, as members came or went, it was to or from other experimental jazz outfits. In 1971 after working on FOUR, Wyatt left once and for all to form the even jazzier Matching Mole. The album FIVE saw Soft Machine moving slightly away from straight jazz and more into jazz-rock territory. SIX became a double album, one disc live and the other in the studio. After spending four years in Soft Machine Hugh Hopper decided it was time to leave. Hopper's replacement was Roy Babbington and the album that followed, SEVEN, was made up of shorter compositions with even less jazz influence.

Noted jazz-rock guitarist Allan Holdsworth joined in the fall of 1973 and took the band in a much rockier direction as evidenced by the 1975 release BUNDLES, the first Soft Machine recording to bear a name and not just a number. Shortly after the album's release he chose to leave and recommended John Etheridge take over the guitarist duties. That seemed to work out well and the band went on a package tour of Europe on the same bill as Caravan and Mahavishnu Orchestra. The tour, fraught with organizational problems, failed to ignite the Softs career and their popularity began to slide. In 1976 Ratledge, who by this time was the sole original member, quit. This left Etheridge, Karl Jenkins (reeds, keyboards), John Marshall (drums), Roy Babbington (bass) and Alan Wakeman (saxes, cousin to Rick Wakeman) to carry on. True to form, the personnel

*Soft Machine*

changes continued as Wakeman stayed for just six months, Babbington left in the summer of 1976 as well. The band released the cryptically titled ALIVE AND WELL IN PARIS in 1978 featuring material pulled from a series of concerts during the spring of the previous year.

The Soft Machine rallied for one more studio effort in 1981 with the lineup consisting of Jenkins, Marshall, a returning Alan Holdsworth and Jack Bruce. The album, entitled LAND OF COCKAYNE, was weak and has been called embarrassing elevator music by some. With a slightly revised lineup the Softs took one last gasp performing a series of gigs at Ronnie Scott's Club in London during 1984. Plans for any further revivals seem doubtful as prime mover Karl Jenkins has since found a far more lucrative career in the field of TV and advertising music.

There's no question that The Soft Machine had a profound impact on bands then and now when it comes to experimenting with the rock genre. They were always challenging and highly creative. Their incorporation of unusual jazz voicings and free-form improvisation influenced many. Soft Machine aficionados are quick to claim their best work occurred on their first four releases.

- THE SOFT MACHINE (1968 Probe)
- VOLUME 2 (1969 Probe)
- THIRD (1970 Columbia)
- FOURTH (1971 Columbia)
- FIVE (1972 Columbia)
- SIX (1972 Columbia)
- 1 & 2 (1973 Probe Compilation)
- SEVEN (1973 Columbia)
- BUNDLES (1975 Harvest)
- SOFTS (1976 Harvest)
- TRIPLE ECHO [BOX SET] (1977 Harvest)
- ALIVE & WELL (1978 Harvest)
- LAND OF COCKAYNE (1981 EMI)
- LIVE AT THE PROMS 1970 (1988 Reckless)
- JET PROPELLED PHOTOGRAPHS (1989 Charly)
- VOLS. 1 & 2 (1989 Big Beat Compilation)
- THE UNTOUCHABLE (1990 Castle Compilation)
- AS IF (1991 Elite Compilation)
- THE PEEL SESSIONS (1991 Strange Fruit)
- BBC RADIO 1 LIVE IN CONCERT #1 (1993 Windsong)
- BBC RADIO 1 LIVE IN CONCERT #2 (1994 Windsong)
- RUBBER RIFF [RECORDED IN 1976] (1995 Voiceprint)
- LIVE IN FRANCE [RECORDED IN 1972] (1995 Oneway)
- LIVE AT THE PARADISO 1969 (1995 Voiceprint)

o SPACED [RECORDED IN 1969] (1996 Cuneiform)
o VIRTUALLY [RECORDED IN 1971] (1997 Cuneiform)
o LIVE 1970 (1998 Voiceprint)

# ~ **43** ~

# Spock's Beard (United States)

They've been hailed as the best American prog band to emerge since the 70's. Spock's Beard create complex symphonic prog with great melodies and lots of time and tempo changes, incorporating piano, organ, Mellotron, guitar, bass and percussion yet sounding very 90's. Musically they have a lot in common with bands such as Echolyn, Crack the Sky, Argent, Yes and Gentle Giant.

Spock's Beard was created in 1992 by brothers Neal and Al Morse. Al had a small home studio and they set out to create music that they liked as opposed to what seemed popular. At the time Neal played keyboards and handled lead vocals while Al worked the guitars, cellos, other stringed instruments and backup vocals. From the very beginning their music consisted of many layers of musical textures, with both guitar and keyboards sharing the spotlight. Like others, they began working in a prog style before realizing the size of the prog underground that existed at the time.

As the compositions progressed the brothers began to focus on the rhythm section and brought in long time friend Dave Meros on bass and vocals. Drumming chores were handled by Nick D'Virgilio, who claims early Genesis as his favourites and who's done session work with Tears For Fears. D'Virgilio appears on the Genesis CALLING ALL STATIONS CD and most recently worked with Peter Gabriel. The final band member to join the fold was Ryo Okumoto, an LA keyboardist who's worked with the likes of Phil Collins and Eric Clapton. He came on after the release of Spock's Beard's first CD, THE LIGHT, released in 1995. In many ways THE LIGHT proved to be a ground breaking album, combining the epic scale compositions of the progressive rock genre with a strong pop / rock sensibility and it won rave reviews around the world.

Spock's Beard's use of instruments includes such prog stalwarts as Hammond organ, Leslie speakers and Mellotrons. And they're used effectively in virtually every composition. That's perhaps one of the trademarks of Spock's Beard, they arrange in force, throwing everything into it.

Compositional inspiration is evident from such bands as Kansas, Styx, Gentle Giant and Genesis, and yet they've assimilated those elements and created a sound that is distinctly their own. A sign of their musical maturity is evident on their first CD with its long multi-part compositions and extremely tight musicianship. Based on the lack of response from the major record labels, the band formed Radiant Records in 1996 to release their future music.

BEWARE OF DARKNESS (1996) shows the band picking up where the first CD left off, only this time as more experienced writers and performers. The compositions are full of tight harmonies, musical precision, multiple times and tempos, and three part contrapuntal composition in both short and long songs. It was every bit progressive rock and yet somehow still accessible. Once again the reviews from around the world were very positive. It was clear that Spock's Beard's unique combination of musical styles was appealing to the prog masses. The Classic Rock Society in Britain named Spock's Beard "Best New Band" in 1996.

KINDNESS OF STRANGERS (1997) demonstrates that sticking with a style can lead to amazing things. Each of the elements heard on their previous recordings is here in spades and sounds better than ever. The playing is tighter, the songs are better constructed and their use of diverse musical styles and instrumentation has increased. Amazing counter play between powerful drumming and thundering bass guitar is counterpointed by the cello and keyboards weaving in and out of each title. In true prog fashion, the album is loosely themed around the state of modern culture. The central theme of the CD is best summed up in a few lines from *The Good Don't Last* which states: "We could've made anything we wanted to make; So we made Wheel of Fortune and all the popular songs; We made a land where crap is king, and the good don't last too long." Again the Classic Rock Society hailed Spock's Beard as "Best Overseas Band" for 1997. Based on the their growing popularity and the glowing reviews the band undertook their first European tour in 1998.

After emptying the vaults with an odds and ends release in early 1999 entitled RARITIES, the band released their new studio CD, DAY FOR NIGHT, displaying once again the immediately identifiable sound they've crafted over the previous six years.

Spock's Beard is one of the most influential prog bands of the 90's bands because of their sudden rise to prominence as well as their overriding desire to make no compromises in their musical direction. Spock's Beard light the path for modern prog hopefuls, artists and fans alike. Their music is one of the most successful blends of everything that sounds great about 70's prog with a totally contemporary 90's musical sensibility.

o THE LIGHT (1995 Radiant)
o BEWARE OF DARKNESS (1996 Radiant)
o OFFICIAL LIVE BOOTLEG (1996 Radiant)
o THE KINDNESS OF STRANGERS (1997 Radiant)
o RARITIES (1998 Radiant)
o DAY FOR NIGHT (1999 Radiant)

# ~ **44** ~

# Strawbs (England)

The Strawbs are considered one of the more distinctive progressive rock bands to emerge out of the British golden era because their roots are based primarily in the English folk world as opposed to the rock world. They started their career known as The Strawberry Hill Boys playing primarily bluegrass music. Formed in 1967 by David Cousins and schoolmate Tony Hooper, the pair performed in a variety of folk clubs around Leicester University and after a few years of playing the folk club circuit they became known simply as The Strawbs. They released a couple of early folk oriented albums, but it wasn't until the 1970 release JUST A COLLECTION OF ANTIQUES AND CURIOS, recorded live in London at Queen Elizabeth Hall, that the press took notice. There was still a distinct folk-ish flavour, but it was augmented by some brilliant keyboard work from newcomer Rick Wakeman. By this time The Strawbs consisted of Cousins (vocals, guitar), Hooper (vocals, guitar), Wakeman (keyboards), Richard Hudson (conga drums, sitar, vocals) and John Ford (bass, vocals.)

Wakeman had joined with Cousins in one of the first serious attempts at creating folk-rock, and their efforts took another small step forward with the 1971 release FROM THE WITCHWOOD. The songs, many haunting in nature due to Cousins unique vocal style, were shorter this time around but they were developing more of an edge. True to their folk roots, the songs dealt with contemporary politics. Wakeman introduced the Mellotron and synthesizer to the band's sound. For all the changes, Wakeman was anxious to do more. It was around this time he received a call from Chris Squire to join Yes, an up-and-coming progressive rock band at the time that more suited Wakeman's musical direction. Wakeman's replacement was Blue Weaver, formerly with the Blues outfit Amen Corner. The new lineup recorded GRAVE NEW WORLD in 1972 and continued their move in a progressive direction. The album's subject matter this time around took in inspirational and spiritual writings dating back many years and the group then applied their own progressive rock slant to the compositions. Weaver incorporated Mellotron on over half of the album's tracks and the band began relying on higher impact staging for their live shows, including special lights and even back projections. This seemed too far removed from their folk roots for Tony Hooper and after The Strawbs played the Chelmsford Folk Festival in 1972 he left. Hooper's replacement was Dave Lambert who brought an even rockier tone to the group.

The Strawbs had had a hit with the tune *Lay Down* and in early 1973 and an even more substantial hit single with *Part of the Union*, a tune from the team of Hudson and Ford. Things seemed to be looking up. In 1973 they released BURSTING AT THE SEAMS, an album where everything came together — the power of the music, strong melodies, and loads of organ and Mellotron creating an orchestral background. And then it all fell apart. Hudson and Ford, never happy with the composing credits agreement, split to go solo and a stressed out Blue Weaver just left. Cousins took a break to rethink what he wanted to do. Lambert stayed on and they pieced together a new unit consisting of, ex-Renaissance John Hawken (keyboards), Chas Cronk (bass) and Rod Coombes (drums.) Together they recorded their most prog effort thus far, HERO AND HEROINE, in 1974, and while it was virtually ignored in England, did quite well in America, a trend that would continue for the band's remaining releases. They followed that up with GHOSTS in 1975 after which Hawken left. With NOMADNESS the following year, they became more a rock band, with folk and slight classical touches here and there, and guest keyboards were handled by John Mealing and Rick Wakeman. For DEEP CUTS the quartet was assisted on keyboards by not only Mealing, but Robert Kirby and Rupert Holmes. Holmes didn't become a permanent fixture but the other two did and went on to record BURNING FOR YOU, and then Tony Fernandez replaced Rod Coombes on drums for a final effort that proved to be somewhat more progressive rock oriented, DEADLINES. The band found themselves fighting a losing battle. These last albums, released during the height of the punk era, never found their way to any media attention and consequently never found an audience. The Strawbs quietly ceased to exist.

In 1983 Cousins received an invitation to play the Cambridge Folk Festival. Under The Strawbs name he then brought together Hooper, Hudson, Ford, Weaver and Brian Willoughby and performed to overwhelming response. The group then even undertook a tour in the states in the mid-80's, which led to two more albums being recorded — DON'T SAY GOODBYE in 1987 and 1991's RINGING DOWN THE YEARS — with more or less the same lineup. The music, by this time having lost much of its progressive rock flavour, took on more of a folk-pop sound, based around Cousins voice and lyrics. Today the band, an ever-changing lineup headed by Dave Cousins, continues to perform in small venues as commitments allow. While their time in the prog limelight was short, Strawbs are included for their efforts at melding folk and rock in a prog context.

o SANDY DENNY & THE STRAWBS: ALL OUR OWN WORK (1968 Hallmark)
o STRAWBS (1969 A&M)
o DRAGONFLY (1970 A&M)
o ANTIQUES AND CURIOUS (1970 A&M)
o FROM THE WITCHWOOD (1971 A&M)
o GRAVE NEW WORLD (1972 A&M)

- BURSTING AT THE SEAMS (1973 A&M)
- HERO AND HEROINE (1974 A&M)
- STRAWBS BY CHOICE (1974 A&M)
- GHOSTS (1975 A&M)
- NOMADNESS (1976 A&M)
- DEEP CUTS (1976 Oyster)
- BURNING FOR YOU (1977 Oyster)
- DEADLINES (1978 Arista)
- BEST OF STRAWBS (1978 A&M)
- DON'T SAY GOODBYE (1987 Toots)
- PRESERVES UNCANNED (1991 Road Goes On Forever)
- RINGING DOWN THE YEARS (1991 Virgin)
- A CHOICE SELECTION OF STRAWBS (1993 A&M)
- GREATEST HITS: LIVE (1993 Road Goes On Forever)
- HEARTBREAK HILL (1995 Road Goes On Forever)
- IN CONCERT (1995 Windsong)
- HALCYON DAYS (1997 A&M)

# ~ 45 ~

# Styx (United States)

Most critics label Styx as America's response to the British progressive rock movement. While this may or may not be the case, they did create some fine music in their early days. That early music consisted of longer compositions, complicated arrangements, and lots of keyboard and guitar interplay. They eventually streamlined their sound and helped create the highly successful arena rock style of AOR music. More than any other prog band, Styx were always able to write successful hit singles and were the first group ever to have four consecutive triple-platinum albums.

Styx had actually been around in one form or another since 1964. The members had been playing in a variety of Chicago bands and finally connected as a unit to record their first LP, STYX I, in 1972. The lineup consisted of Chuck Panozzo (bass), John Panozzo (drums), Dennis DeYoung (keyboards), John Curulewski (guitar) and James Young (guitar.) Originally known as The Tradewinds, the record company encouraged them to find a new name. The band settled on Styx. From the outset they proved themselves capable of tackling a variety of musical styles. Ballads came easy but they could rock out just as easily and, most importantly

for prog fans, was the fact they were also able to create more adventurous material like their thirteen minute multi-part *Movement for the Common Man.* Their third LP released in 1973, THE SERPENT IS RISING, contained long tracks with innovative use of the classics, albeit in a somewhat rockier environment than most British progressive rock bands. The album closer, *Krakatoa,* leads into an exhilarating rock enhanced version of Handel's *Hallelujah Chorus.* The band toured extensively between each release and even kept day jobs for a number of years.

The big break for Styx came when a Chicago radio station played their song *Lady* every night until it became a hit, finally reaching a top ten spot two years after it was originally released.

Unhappy with their record company, they took the opportunity to seek out a better deal and landed with A&M which released EQUINOX in 1975. Just as the band was about to leave on tour, Curulewski left. His replacement for the tour was Tommy Shaw. Needless to say, Shaw worked out so well that he was invited to stay on as a permanent member of Styx and his guitar work was very evident on their next release, CRYSTAL BALL in 1976. The touring continued with Styx performing almost 400 dates over the next two years. By this time their fan base was growing outside of the U.S. as well, and in 1977 they released THE GRAND ILLUSION. Each album went from strength to strength and seemed to capture the prevailing musical moment. The playing got better, and each album also contained hit singles, such as *Come Sail Away* and *Fooling Yourself*, which propelled the band further up the popularity ladder.

In actual fact the next three albums — PIECES OF EIGHT (1978), CORNERSTONE (1979) and PARADISE THEATER (1980) — continued the band's successful track record even as they moved more away from progressive rock. The band managed to keep writing hits, such as *Babe*, *Too Much Time on My Hands* and *The Best of Times*, and continued to hang on to just enough prog tendencies to keep the music interesting to their older fans.

With PARADISE THEATER the band ventured into, if not a concept album, certainly one tied together thematically, as all the compositions dealt with the condition of the country, the human condition and even conditions of the heart. In fact, it turned out to be their first and only number one album. Taking that one stage further, they went into the studio to create KILROY WAS HERE, which included not only the sound concept but a complete multimedia package for touring. After yet another massive tour, the band, totally exhausted, decided to take a long extended break. All members got involved in solo projects or worked with others in a more casual environment.

Six years later they reformed, minus Shaw whose commitments kept him elsewhere, and in late 1989 released EDGE OF THE CENTURY. Even after all that time away, the band demonstrated that they were still able to craft successful singles — such as *Show Me the Way* which climbed to No. 3 on the charts — making Styx one of only a small handful of bands to have Top 10 hits over three decades. After another successful tour throughout 1991 the band went their separate ways again.

They regrouped in 1996 for a highly successful Return To Paradise Tour of the States and it's subsequent double CD release which included three new tracks. Encouraged by the success of the tour the band made plans to work on a new album.

- o STYX I (1972 RCA)
- o STYX II (1973 RCA)
- o THE SERPENT IS RISING (1973 RCA)
- o MAN OF MIRACLES (1974 RCA)

- EQUINOX (1975 A&M)
- CRYSTAL BALL (1976 A&M)
- THE GRAND ILLUSION (1977 A&M)
- PIECES OF EIGHT (1978 A&M)
- CORNERSTONE (1979 A&M)
- PARADISE THEATER (1980 A&M)
- KILROY WAS HERE (1983 A&M)
- CAUGHT IN THE ACT (1984 A&M)
- STYX CLASSICS VOL. 15 (1987 A&M)
- EDGE OF THE CENTURY (1992 A&M)
- GREATEST HITS (1995 A&M)
- GREATEST HITS PART 2 (1996 A&M)
- RETURN TO PARADISE (1997 CMC International)

# ~ 46 ~
# Tangerine Dream (Germany)

Formed in 1967 as a rock band, Tangerine Dream remained virtually unknown until the advent of the Moog Synthesizer, which changed their whole musical focus. They are, without question, one of the founding electronic bands to come out of the space-rock genre. Their early music exhibited the droning-endless-looping elements of space-rock; their mid period tends to incorporate more rhythmic sequencer pieces; and their later work includes shorter song based material.

The original trio consisted of Edgar Froese (keyboards, guitar), Klaus Schulze (keyboards) and Konrad Schnitzler (keyboards) and their first album, ELECTRONIC MEDITATION, was released in 1970, already showing them eschewing the conventions of traditional rock and roll in favour of a more improvised sound. The first of many personnel changes took place shortly after the album's release. The new lineup of Froese, Christoph Franke (keyboards, drums) and Peter Baumann (keyboards) released three more albums before changing labels and signing with Virgin Records. Having already established a sizable following, their first two Virgin LPs — PHAEDRA (1974) and RUBYCON (1975) — managed a respectable showing on the British album charts.

The group in 1974 played a concert at Rheims Cathedral where almost 6,000 fans tried to squeeze into the 2,000 available seats. This set a trend for Tangerine

Dream, who took the opportunity to play in these typically gothic settings as often as possible. During the sellout 1975 British tour they played York Minster and Coventry and Liverpool Cathedrals along with a host of other venues. The live album, RICOCHET, included performances culled from the successful tour.

Up until this point, their music had been spacey, with long droning passages, and floating synths rolling over syncopated rhythms. For the 1976 release STRATOSPHERE, they changed their approach and included other traditional instruments and began developing stronger melodies for their compositions. This was a big year for the band as they undertook their first tour of the United States, and it also signaled the beginnings of Tangerine Dream's long running association with the creation of movie soundtracks, including work on THE EXORCIST, THE FRENCH CONNECTION and THE SORCERER.

In 1977 the band undertook a second tour of the United States. Unfortunately, it was cut short as a result of a riding accident which put Froese out of commission. The band suffered another blow a little while later when Baumann left to develop his solo career. Baumann would later become influential in the development of synth / keyboard talent with the creation of his Private Music Label. Tangerine Dream regrouped and Froese and Franke added Steve Joliffe (vocals, keyboards, wind instruments) and Klaus Kriefer (drums) and then recorded CYCLONE. The vocals resulted in mixed reviews and the band spent most of 1979 working on solo projects, but in between found time to record FORCE MAJEURE.

After almost a year of discussion and negotiations, Tangerine Dream became the first Western rock band to perform in East Germany. While performing there they came into contact with Johannes Schmoelling who joined and made his first recorded debut on the 1980 release TANGRAM. They continued for the next few years as a trio. In 1981 they created another movie soundtrack for the film THIEF and the album EXIT. By this time Tangerine Dream had developed a very different style. While still incorporating their layers of synths and droning soundscapes, they were now underpinning the whole affair was a very serious driving rhythm, which borrowed from the techno-pop of the day and incorporated the latest in hi-tech synth sequencers. After 1985's LE PARC, Schmoelling went off to pursue a solo career and was replaced by Paul Haslinger. By this time Tangerine Dream were composing as many, if not more, movie soundtracks per year as mainstream recordings. Fortunately for a band like Tangerine Dream the compositional styles are so similar the fans are the true winners.

After many years together, a difference of musical direction arose between Froese and Franke. Froese and Haslinger continued working on personal material as well as soundtracks for the next couple years until Haslinger also decided to leave allowing Froese's son Jerome to join the band. In 1995 father and son under the Tangerine Dream name set about remixing some of their earlier material under the title THE DREAM MIXES, which ended up sitting on the new age music charts. The latest phase of Tangerine Dream looks set to continue the musical aspirations of Edgar Froese for some time to come. Their more recent work has tended to focus on shorter, more rhythmic compositions, even so, Tangerine Dream continue to command a devoted fan following due in large part to their earlier pioneering efforts.

- ELECTRONIC MEDITATION (1970 Ohr)
- ALPHA CENTAURI (1971 Ohr)
- ZEIT (1972 Ohr)
- ATEM (1972 Ohr)
- PHAEDRA (1974 Virgin)
- RUBYCON (1975 Virgin)
- RICOCHET (1976 Virgin)
- STRATOSFEAR (1976 Virgin)
- SORCERER [SOUNDTRACK] (1977 MCA)
- ENCORE (1977 Virgin)
- CYCLONE (1978 Virgin)
- FORCE MAJEURE (1978 Virgin)
- QUICHOTTE — LIVE IN EAST BERLIN (1980 AMIGA)
- TANGRAM (1980 Virgin)
- TANGERINE DREAM 70-80 [BOX SET] (1980 Virgin)
- THIEF [VIOLENT STREETS, SOUNDTRACK] (1981 Virgin)
- EXIT (1981 Virgin)
- WHITE EAGLE (1982 Virgin)
- LOGO — LIVE AT THE DOMINION (1983 Virgin)
- WAVELENGTH [SOUNDTRACK] (1983 Varese Sarabande)
- HYPERBOREA (1983 Virgin)
- RISKY BUSINESS [SOUNDTRACK] (1983 Virgin)
- POLAND — THE WARSAW CONCERT (1984 Castle)
- FIRESTARTER [SOUNDTRACK] (1984 Varese Sarabande)
- FLASHPOINT [SOUNDTRACK] (1984 EMI America)
- LE PARC (1985 Castle)
- HEARTBREAKERS [SOUNDTRACK] (1985 Virgin)
- LEGEND [SOUNDTRACK] (1985 MCA)
- DREAM SEQUENCE (1985 Virgin Compilation)
- PERGAMON — LIVE (1985 Castle)
- IN THE BEGINNING [BOX SET] (1986 Zomba)
- GREEN DESERT [RECORDED IN 1973] (1986 Castle)
- UNDERWATER SUNLIGHT (1986 Castle)
- THE COLLECTION (1987 Castle Compilation)
- TYGER (1987 Castle)

- NEAR DARK [SOUNDTRACK] (1987 Silva Screen)
- THREE O'CLOCK HIGH [SOUNDTRACK] (1987 Varese Sarabande)
- SHY PEOPLE [SOUNDTRACK] (Varese Sarabande)
- LIVE MILES (1988 Castle)
- DEAD SOLID PERFECT [SOUNDTRACK] (1988 Silva Screen)
- OPTICAL RACE (1988 Private Music)
- LILY ON THE BEACH (1989 Private Music)
- MIRACLE MILE [SOUNDTRACK] (1989 Private Music)
- MELROSE (1990 Private Music)
- DESTINATION BERLIN [SOUNDTRACK] (1990 BMG)
- THE MAN INSIDE [SOUNDTRACK] (1991 EMI)
- CANYON DREAMS [SOUNDTRACK] (1991 Miramar)
- ROCKON (1992 Miramar)
- DEADLY CARE [SOUNDTRACK] (1992 Silva Screen)
- 220 VOLT LIVE (1993 Miramar)
- TURN OF THE TIDES (1994 Miramar)
- CATCH ME IF YOU CAN [SOUNDTRACK] (1994 Edel America)
- TANGENTS 1973-83 (1994 Capitol)
- DREAM MUSIC [SOUNDTRACKS] (1994 Silva Screen Compilation)
- TRYANNY OF BEAUTY (1995 Miramar)
- ZONING [SOUNDTRACK] (1995 Repertoire Records)
- THE DREAM MIXES (1995 Miramar)
- THE DREAM MIXES SPECIAL (1996 TDI Music)
- GOBLINS CLUB (1996 Castle)
- OASIS [SOUNDTRACK] (1997 TDI Music)
- TOURNADO LIVE (1997 TDI Music)
- TIMESQUARE — DREAM MIXES II (1997 TDI Music)
- THE KEEP [SOUNDTRACK] (1997 TDI Music)
- AMBIENT MONKEYS (1997 TDI Music)

# ~ **47** ~

# UK (England)

UK came on the scene at the tail end of 70's when everyone had pretty much given up on progressive rock. And yet, with even their short time on the scene, UK made a significant impact. These were high profile musicians creating music that was imaginative, intelligent and boundary stretching progressive rock. And even more amazing was the fact that there was an audience out there who wanted to hear it. Their music was powerful and challenging, juxtaposing inventive rhythms, shifting textures and moving melodies within a framework that remained direct and accessible. UK were nothing short of brilliant.

The band started life as a trio of Bill Bruford (drums), Eddie Jobson (violin, keyboards), and John Wetton (vocals, bass), and after a search for a guitarist they decided on Allan Holdsworth. Their cumulative years of prog experience is staggering. Just a quick overview shows Bill Bruford having been in Yes, King Crimson and Genesis; Eddie Jobson with Curved Air, Roxy Music, and Frank Zappa; John Wetton with King Crimson, Family, Roxy Music and even Uriah Heep. This "star" lineup released the first self-titled album in the spring of 1978 and it met with critical and commercial success. The band immediately set out on tour both in Britain and America. They played to standing ovations and the band's hard hitting orchestral sound was drawing rave reviews.

UK's original plan was to return to the studio and record a second album as soon as possible. Trouble was, the demand for live appearances was so high that they were forced to return to the U.S. on a headlining tour, which kept them on the road until late 1978. In part due to the proposed heavy touring schedule, both Bruford and Holdsworth departed after the first LP and UK became a trio once again by adding former Zappa drummer Terry Bozzio. In fact, the future of UK was never in doubt because a quick scan of the composing credits showed that virtually all of the material on the first album had been written by the team of Wetton and Jobson. They were the ones who set the tone for the band's sound and musical direction. The revised trio entered the studio in late 1978 and began work on their next recording.

DANGER MONEY was released in 1979 and displayed a more direct progressive rock style. There was less of a jazz influence and more of a rock-orientation. This slight shift in approach resulted in drawing even more fans. It wasn't long before UK was back on the road again, and it was during the Japanese leg of the tour that they recorded the live performances which became their next LP, NIGHT AFTER NIGHT. It even included two new songs, once again from the hands of Wetton and Jobson.

The band looked poised to take progressive rock music into the 80's. However, it was not to be. They broke up shortly after the completion of the tour. The progressive rock banner was taken up by others — some inspired by the success of UK. Eddie Jobson landed in Jethro Tull for their 1980 release A, while John Wetton went on to create Asia.

Nothing was heard from UK for over a decade. Then, in the mid 90's, rumours started to circulate that UK were getting back together again. The rumours turned into fact when it was announced that John Wetton and Eddie Jobson were once again working together on new material to be released under the UK name. Apparently, much of the material had been completed but was stalled under Jobson's quest for perfection. Unhappy with how long production was taking, Wetton announced in 1998 he was leaving the project. Jobson proclaimed that the material was still being worked on and would probably be released with Wetton's presence on the tracks, but probably not under the UK name. The legacy of this short-lived band lives on.

Their use of textures and moods in the songs, produced over a too-short career, out shone much of the other music released on vinyl at the time. This was a supergroup just as Asia was to become. Only, with UK the music remained important. They created more than just some nice catchy songs. It seemed that success, if it came, would be nice, but the band determined to soldier on despite the lack of radio airplay. The crowds loved them live. They challenged all the critics by bucking the trend and creating imaginative, intelligent, boundary stretching progressive rock. Their music contained all the prog hallmarks of inventive rhythms, shifting textures and tempos and moving melodies. UK was one of the premier bands of the late 70's and helped form the bridge to the progressive rock bands of the 80's.

- UK (1978 EG Records)
- DANGER MONEY (1979 EG Records)
- NIGHT AFTER NIGHT (1979 EG Records)
- IN THE DEAD OF NIGHT [LIVE IN 1979] (1997 Independent)

# ~ **48** ~

# Van Der Graaf Generator (England)

One of the bands to exist almost exclusively on a loyal cult following was Van Der Graaf Generator. Led by Peter Hammill, the group went through many personnel changes and incorporated an eclectic assortment of instruments, although lead guitar was only adopted full time late in their career. Van Der Graaf borrowed from jazz, classical, electronic and blues to create their own brand of prog. They were also one of the few prog rock bands to incorporate saxophone into the lineup.

Van Der Graaf was formed in 1967 by Peter Hammill when he met up with Chris Smith and Nick Pearn as students at Manchester University. Given the spontaneous nature of the music business at the time, they played a few solo gigs, played support for T Rex, Marc Bolen's group, and then were quickly signed to a recording contract. In short order, Hugh Banton, a classical trained organist, replaced Pearn, Guy Evans came in on drums and Keith Ellis on bass. Around this time, they picked up a new manager in the person of Tony Stratton Smith, released their first single, and suffered the loss of Chris Smith. The band soldiered on and secured a support spot with Jimi Hendrix at the Royal Albert Hall. Unfortunately, after the gig, their equipment was stolen. Demoralized, they threw in the towel and called it a day.

With little future in sight for the band, Hammill decided to record a solo album, which eventually became the group's first LP. Calling upon Banton, Evans and Ellis, they recorded THE AEROSOL GREY MACHINE after which Ellis left to join the blues oriented Juicy Lucy and was replaced by Nic Porter. Hammill then recruited David Jackson and Van Der Graaf began work on their second album, to be released on Tony Stratton Smith's new label Charisma. The resulting album was entitled THE LEAST WE CAN DO IS WAVE TO EACH OTHER. Van Der Graaf then joined label mates Genesis and Lindisfarne for a series of intensive tours that took them to virtually every part of Britain. Following the tour, the band was back in the studio, but before completing their next album Porter left. Robert Fripp, who had recently declined an invitation to join Yes, agreed to do guest guitar work and the album H TO HE WHO AM THE ONLY was released in 1970. The band again took off on tour, this time performing on the continent where they amassed quite a following, particularly in Italy.

In 1971 Hammill recorded his first true solo album entitled FOOL'S MATE with

many of the band participating. A few months later Van Der Graaf recorded their next release, PAWN HEARTS, once again with Robert Fripp's assistance on guitar. Many fans and critics alike consider PAWN HEARTS, with its challenging twenty three minute epic *A Plague of Lighthouse Keepers*, the band's masterpiece of progressive rock music. The album went straight to No. 1 on the Italian music charts and Van Der Graaf were riding the wave of success. Unfortunately, they were also exhausted after countless tours and decided to call it a day. Hammill picked up on what has become a very prolific solo recording career. At last count Hammill was responsible for over 25 solo releases.

At the request of fans and promoters, the band agreed to reform in 1975 with Hammill, Banton, Evans and Jackson and, after a brief tour in France, recorded GODBLUFF. Feeling that their material had become too complex, GODBLUFF showed the band composing and performing in a more streamlined fashion. The music was more direct and to a degree rockier, less intricate. Hammill was now playing electric guitar, Jackson's electric saxophone setup was improved and Banton had built a new type of organ. It all felt good and the band went on to record STILL LIFE and WORLD RECORD in 1976. A series of support tours followed and in the end Banton and Jackson decided to leave. The pressures of life on the road simply became too much and they chose to quit music as full time careers. Hammill brought in replacements Graham Smith and Nick Porter. The band shorted their name to Van Der Graaf and, with the new lineup and sound, they recorded THE QUIET ZONE / THE PLEASURE DOME in 1977. The saxophone was now replaced with a solo electric violin played by Smith. Adding yet another new member, Charles Dickie came in on cello and keyboards, Van Der Graaf recorded a gig at London's Marquee Club which resulted in VITAL / VAN DER GRAAF LIVE. The group undertook a two month tour of Europe and then split for the final time, playing its last concert in 1978. Hammill chose to concentrate on his solo career as the outlet for his creativity, although from time to time he continued to work with former band members.

While they were critically well received, they never really won the popular acclaim of the "big six". Their early material was full of a jagged-edged prog with many signature changes and complicated arrangements. Much has been written about Hammill's unique vocal style with its emotion laden delivery. Suffice it to say, if you'd like to know who David Bowie looked to for vocal inspiration, look no further than Hammill. Van Der Graaf are a band easily recommended to fans of Gentle Giant, or even Genesis, who might be looking for something a little more edgy.

- AEROSOL GREY MACHINE (1969 Mercury)
- THE LEAST WE CAN DO IS WAVE TO EACH OTHER (1970 Probe)
- H TO HE WHO AM THE ONLY ONE (1970 ABC/Dunhill)
- PAWN HEARTS (1971 Charisma)
- 68-71 (1972 Charisma Compilation)
- GODBLUFF (1975 Charisma)
- STILL LIFE (1976 Charisma)
- WORLD RECORD (1976 Charisma)
- THE QUIET ZONE / THE PLEASURE DOME (1977 Charisma)
- ROCK HEAVIES — VAN DER GRAAF GENERATOR (1977 Charisma Compilation)
- VITAL — VAN DER GRAAF LIVE (1978 Charisma)
- REPEAT PERFORMANCE (1980 Charisma Compilation)
- TIME VAULTS (1985 Demi-Monde)
- FIRST GENERATION (1986 Virgin Compilation)
- SECOND GENERATION (1986 Virgin Compilation)
- I PROPHECY DISASTER (1993 Virgin Comp + Rare Tracks)
- MAIDA VALE (1994 Band of Joy Live Compilation)
- THE MASTERS (1998 Eagle Compilation)

# ~ **49** ~

# Wakeman, Rick (England)

Rick Wakeman is probably the most well known keyboardist in the world of progressive rock music and, together with Keith Emerson, is responsible for creating the prog keyboard ethic which incorporated banks of keyboards played simultaneously. Always bearing the brunt of critic's abuse, Wakeman came on the scene with formal music schooling from The Royal College of Music. During his time at college, Wakeman got involved with session work and pub gigs as a creative outlet. Soon, the outside interests got in the way of schooling and Wakeman left the college without a degree. In the late 60's, without school to attend to, he could focus more on the studio work and began working on sessions with Cat Stevens, T. Rex and David Bowie. For example; the Mellotron solo during Bowie's *Space Odyssey* was pure Wakeman. In early 1970 he joined up with David Cousins and Strawbs in an effort to take folk music to the next level. Both Cousins and Wakeman wanted to chart new territory by introducing a more electric element to folk music, as well as write material that drew on other influences. Their idea was to create the first true folk-rock band. To this end, Wakeman's influence can clearly be heard on their 1971 release FROM THE WITCHWOOD. Wakeman remained with The Strawbs for a few years and on his last tour with them they played in support of Yes, where Chris Squire had the opportunity to see Wakeman's style in action. After the tour, Wakeman decided he'd had enough of bands and was going to concentrate on session work. Shortly thereafter, he received a middle of the night phone call from Chris Squire to come and join Yes. Wakeman originally declined, but in the end joined creating one of the most creatively explosive band lineups ever. Their first LP, FRAGILE, helped establish the genre of progressive rock. For Wakeman it was the chance of a lifetime, participating in the creation of music that went beyond the pop norms.

In the early 1973, while still with Yes, Wakeman began his prolific solo career with the release of THE SIX WIVES OF HENRY VIII. While the album's musical interpretations of Henry's six wives helped form an outlet for Wakeman's musical virtuosity, it did nothing to quell his sense of spectacle. That he accomplished with the live recording of his second album in 1974, JOURNEY TO THE CENTRE OF THE EARTH. This album, recorded with full orchestra and narrator, went to No. 1 on the UK charts and No. 3 in the United States. Not satisfied, he went one step further in 1976 and recorded THE MYTHS AND LEGENDS OF KING ARTHUR, again with full orchestra, and then proceeded to stage the entire live event, complete with actors on ice, with his own band, The English Rock Ensemble. He ended up losing a fortune on such events. Around this time Wakeman got involved in creating movie soundtracks, the first of which was the Ken Russell film LISZTOMANIA, in which he also played the part of a Marvel comics-looking Norse god Thor. He also began diversifying his interests and, at one point, was the director of 11 different companies. He continued recording solo material, but having been burned by the grand scale of his earlier works, the albums released through the rest of his career tended to be more modest and concise.

Wakeman was one of the first artists to get involved with the creation of new age music with the release of a solo piano album entitled COUNTRY AIRS in 1986. As a Christian, his involvement with the new age only goes as far as the music however, and he has consistently contributed releases to this genre as well as others, such as his gospel or religious recordings. The advent of cheaper recording and CD technology has allowed Wakeman to become even more prolific, releasing as many as three or four CD's in one year. In addition, he's become more involved with his keyboard playing son Adam, and the two have released a number of CD's performing together. Over the years, Wakeman has returned to the Yes fold a number of times, only to leave each time under trying circumstances. The members seem drawn together and yet unable to make it last comfortably. His most recent efforts included the 1997 releases KEYS TO ASCENSION 1 & 2 which, by Wakeman's estimation, contained some of the best Yes music ever. Sadly, management got in the way and Wakeman issued a statement that he probably would never be able to work with Yes again. Only time will tell of course.

Coming full circle, the classical division of EMI approached Wakeman with the idea of doing a sequel to JOURNEY TO THE CENTRE OF THE EARTH. After many meetings and much negotiation, the deal was struck, and in 1999 RETURN TO THE CENTRE OF THE EARTH, with full symphony orchestra and Patrick Stewart as narrator, was released to a flood of publicity. Nearly twice as long as the original, the new recording featured performances from Ozzie Osbourne, Justin Hayward and Trevor Rabin. Needless to say, the music industry is much more cynical in the 90's and reviews were mixed, but that's never stopped Wakeman in the past.

o SIX WIVES OF HENRY THE VIII (1973 A&M)
o JOURNEY TO THE CENTRE OF THE EARTH (1974 A&M)
o MYTHS AND LEGENDS OF KING ARTHUR (1975 A&M)
o LISZTOMANIA [SOUNDTRACK] (1975 A&M)
o NO EARTHLY CONNECTION (1976 A&M)
o WHITE ROCK [SOUNDTRACK] (1976 A&M)
o CRIMINAL RECORD (1977 A&M)
o RHAPSODIES (1979 A&M)

- 1984 (1981 Charisma)
- ROCK "N" ROLL PROPHET (1982 Moon)
- THE BURNING (1982 Varese Sarabande)
- G'OLE [SOUNDTRACK] (1982 Charisma)
- THE COST OF LIVING (1983 Charisma)
- LYTTON'S DIARY [SOUNDTRACK] (1985 President)
- SILENT NIGHTS (1985 TBG President)
- LIVE AT THE HAMMERSMITH (1985 President)
- CRIMES OF PASSION [SOUNDTRACK] (1986 President)
- COUNTRY AIRS (1986 Coda Records)
- THE GOSPELS (1987 Stylus)
- THE FAMILY ALBUM (1987 President)
- A SUITE OF GODS (1987 President)
- 20th ANNIVERSARY LIMITED EDITION (1988 President)
- TIME MACHINE (1988 President)
- ZODIAQUE (1988 President)
- SEA AIRS (1989 President)
- BLACK KNIGHTS AT THE COURT OF FERDINAND IV (1989 Ambient)
- PHANTOM POWER (1990 Ambient)
- IN THE BEGINNING (1990 Asaph Records)
- NIGHT AIRS (1990 President)
- ROCK AND ROLL PROPHET PLUS (1991 President)
- THE CLASSICAL CONNECTION (1991 President)
- ASPIRANT SUNSET (1991 President)
- ASPIRANT SUNRISE (1991 President)
- ASPIRANT SHADOWS (1991 President)
- SOFTSWORD (1991 President)
- 2000 AD IN THE FUTURE (1991 President)
- AFRICAN BACH (1991 President)
- COUNTRY AIRS (1992 President)
- BEST WORKS COLLECTION (1992 Jimco Records)
- UNLEASHING THE TETHERED ONE — THE 1974 NORTH AMERICAN TOUR (1993 Mellow Records)
- CLASSIC TRACKS (1993 Zazoo)
- PRAYERS (1993 Hope Records)
- THE HERITAGE SUITE (1993 President)
- WAKEMAN WITH WAKEMAN (1993 President)
- THE CLASSICAL CONNECTION 2 (1993 President)
- NO EXPENSE SPARED (1993 President)
- LURE OF THE WILD (1994 Mota Blu Musica)
- THE STAGE COLLECTION (1994 Mota Blu Musica)
- WAKEMAN WITH WAKEMAN LIVE, THE OFFICIAL BOOTLEG (1994 Cyclops)
- RICK WAKEMAN'S GREATEST HITS (1994 Herald)

- LIGHT UP THE SKY (1994 President)
- LIVE ON THE TEST (1994 Windsong)
- WAKEMAN WITH WAKEMAN LIVE (1994 Zero)
- KING BISCUIT FLOWER HOUR PRESENTS RICK WAKEMAN (1995 KBFH Records)
- CIRQUE SURREAL (1995 Pinnacle)
- THE PIANO ALBUM (1995 Castle)
- THE PRIVATE COLLECTION (1995 President)
- ALMOST LIVE IN EUROPE (1995 Griffin)
- ROCK & POP LEGEND — RICK WAKEMAN (1995 Disky)
- ROMANCE OF THE VICTORIAN AGE (1995 President)
- THE 7 WONDERS OF THE WORLD (1995 President)
- VISIONS (1995 President)
- VOYAGE (1996 A&M)
- RICK WAKEMAN'S GREATEST HITS (1996 Disky)
- FIELDS OF GREEN (1996 Griffin)
- TAPESTRIES (1996 President)
- THE WORD AND MUSIC (1996 Hope Records)
- ORISONS (1996 Hope Records)
- CAN YOU HEAR ME (1996 Hope Records)
- VIGNETTES (1996 President)
- THE NEW GOSPELS (1996 Hope Records)
- WELCOME A STAR (1996 Hope Records)
- SIMPLY ACOUSTIC — THE MUSIC (1997 Asaph Records)
- TRIBUTE (1997 RP Media)
- FIELDS OF GREEN '97 (1997 Music Fusion)
- RICK WAKEMAN MASTER SERIES (1998 A&M)
- THEMES (1998 President)
- THE MASTERS (1999 Eagle Records)
- RETURN TO THE CENTRE OF THE EARTH (1999 EMI)

# ~ **50** ~
# Yes (England)

As one of the "Big Six", Yes helped create the progressive rock genre with their mixture of musical styles, superb musicianship, adventurous song writing and the desire to stretch musically. Yes blended the majesty of symphonic prog with the delicacies of acoustic piano and classical guitar. Shunning singles, they were more interested in what they could accomplish using the whole album. Their goal was to create music that would become the classical music of its day and for the future.

They came together in 1968 as Tony Kaye (keyboards), Jon Anderson (vocals), Chris Squire (bass), Bill Bruford (drums) and Peter Banks (guitar), and their first self-titled album, YES, in 1969 just hinted at what was to come. Pooling the contemporary influences of bands like The Nice, The Beatles and even The Fifth Dimension, Yes' music was rife with movie themes, classical influences and elaborate arrangements. The second album, TIME AND A WORD, came out in 1970 after which Peter Banks left to form Flash. His replacement was Steve Howe who quickly established a new guitar sound for the group. Howe's goal had been to get involved with a band interested in elaborate arrangements. It all came together for Yes when, in 1971, they hooked up with producer Eddie Offord and created the landmark LP THE YES ALBUM, which contained the classics *Starship Trooper*, and *Yours Is No Disgrace*. Soon after, the band saw even more potential to shape their symphonic sound if only Tony Kaye would incorporate more keyboards with newer technology. Frustrated, Kaye left and was replaced by Rick Wakeman and together they created progressive rock masterpieces such as FRAGILE, CLOSE TO THE EDGE and TALES OF TOPOGRAPHIC OCEANS. All charted new territory and set the standard for symphonic prog bands.

Bill Bruford, looking for a new challenge, left after CLOSE TO THE EDGE and went with King Crimson. His replacement was Alan White. Wakeman, unhappy with the volume of new material on TALES, left the band to focus on his developing solo career. His replacement was another technically proficient keyboard wizard by the name of Patrick Moraz with whom they recorded RELAYER. For whatever reason, Moraz never really meshed with the rest of the group and left after one album making room for Wakeman's return on the very satisfying GOING FOR THE ONE in 1977. Less than satisfying however, was their next release TORMATO, a very disconnected and rambling LP that resulted in both Anderson and Wakeman leaving.

copyright 1999 Julie Wilson / I S Entertainment

The most unusual period of the band's career occurred next when Chris Squire and manager Brian Lane enlisted the support of then fast rising pop stars The Buggles, namely Trevor Horn and Geoff Downes, to becomes part of the band. The album that resulted, DRAMA, showed a stripped down Yes, not quite as heavily arranged and perhaps a little more edgy. But the formation didn't last and it was three years before the next Yes album. Geoff Downes and Steve Howe went off to form Asia, Trevor Horn went back to producing, and Squire and White attempted a couple of solo projects. The next time Yes got together it consisted of Squire, White, Anderson, original keyboardist Tony Kaye and newcomer Trevor Rabin on guitar. The album 90125 contained the chart topping hit *Owner of a Lonely Heart* and its success once again made Yes a household name. This version of Yes was even more stripped down and less arranged than ever. Yet it was successful and led to the more aggressive BIG GENERATOR in 1987. Towards the

copyright 1999 Julie Wilson / I S Entertainment

end of the 90's, original members Anderson, Bruford, Wakeman and Howe got together under that name and recorded an album of very Yes-sounding material and toured in support. With two versions of Yes on the road, management conceived of the idea of putting the two together. The resulting album, UNION in 1991, is a blend of two very different sounding bands. While everyone put on a good front, the tour was taxing for the many egos involved and all members left disheartened.

In 1994 the Rabin-led Yes recorded their best music on TALK, including the fifteen minute epic *Endless Dream*, but after twelve years in the band, Rabin announced his departure. This cleared the way for a reuniting of Anderson, Squire, Howe, White and Wakeman and the resulting KEYS TO ASCENSION 1 & 2, containing their best music since CLOSE TO THE EDGE — powerful yet delicate; topical yet utopian. Yes were back, or so it seemed. Sadly, management got in the way, forcing Rick Wakeman to leave. The remaining members regrouped and brought in their producer Billy Sherwood to sing and handle keyboards. The first CD with this lineup was a major disappointment. OPEN YOUR EYES in 1997 consisted of mostly shorter, more streamlined songs that lacked the prog flavour of KEYS TO ASCENSION. Recognizing this lack, in their characteristic "never say die" attitude, the band spent much of 1999 in the studio working on new material and promised a return to stronger, more progressive compositions with their next CD.

- YES (1969 Atlantic)
- TIME AND A WORD (1970 Atlantic)
- THE YES ALBUM (1971 Atlantic)
- FRAGILE (1972 Atlantic)
- CLOSE TO THE EDGE (1972 Atlantic)
- YESSONGS (1973 Atlantic)
- TALES FROM TOPOGRAPHIC OCEANS (1974 Atlantic)
- RELAYER (1974 Atlantic)
- YESTERDAYS (1975 Atlantic)
- GOING FOR THE ONE (1977 Atlantic)
- TORMATO (1978 Atlantic)
- YESSHOWS (1980 Atlantic)
- DRAMA (1980 Atlantic)
- CLASSIC YES (1982 Atlantic)
- 90125 (1983 Atlantic)
- 90125 LIVE THE SOLOS (1985 Atlantic)
- BIG GENERATOR (1987 Atlantic)
- UNION (1991 Arista)
- YESYEARS (1991)
- YESSTORY (1991)
- HIGHLIGHTS: THE VERY BEST OF YES (1993)
- TALK (1994 Victory)
- KEYS TO ASCENSION (1996 CMC International)
- SOMETHING'S COMING (1997)
- KEYS TO ASCENSION 2 (1997)
- OPEN YOUR EYES (1997 Beyond Music)

THE NATIONAL JAZZ FEDERATION PRESENTS THE

# 9TH NATIONAL JAZZ BLUES FESTIVAL

TRAVEL: By road about 45 miles from London. Take A23 or A22(A275) turning off at B2116. Special Southern Region Trains. SPECIAL LATE SERVICE back to Victoria and Brighton.

**Friday 8th August** ☐ 8 - 11.30 p m
**THE PINK FLOYD** Tickets 15/-
**SOFT MACHINE**
EAST OF EDEN · BLOSSOM TOES
**Keith Tippett Jazz Group**
JUNIORS EYES · THE VILLAGE

**Saturday 9th August** ☐ 2 Sessions
☐ Afternoon 2 - 5.30 p m Tickets 10/-
**BONZO DOG BAND**
**Roy Harper** · THE STRAWBS
BREAKTHRU' · JIGSAW
PETER HAMMILL

☐ Evening 7 - 11.30 pm
**THE WHO** Tickets £1
**CHICKEN SHACK**
**FAT MATTRESS**
The Jazz Sound of **JOHN SURMAN**
**AYNSLEY DUNBAR** · **YES!**
The Spirit of **JOHN MORGAN**
KING CRIMSON · GROUNDHOGS
DRY ICE · Introducing from Belgium
THE WALLACE COLLECTION

**Sunday 10th August** ☐ 2 Sessions
☐ Afternoon 2 - 5.30 p m Tickets 10/-
**THE PENTANGLE**
**Long John Baldry**
RON GEESIN · JO-ANN KELLY
MAGNA CARTA · NOEL MURPHY

☐ Evening 7 - 11.30 pm Tickets £1
**THE NICE** · **THE FAMILY**
**London Cast of 'HAIR'**
**KEEF HARTLEY · ECLECTION**
**CHRIS BARBER**   Mick
**Abrahams' BLODWYN PIG**
CIRCUS · HARD MEAT · Introducing
from Holland **CUBY'S BLUES BAND**
BABYLON · AFFINITY

**SPECIAL TICKETS** (IN ADVANCE ONLY)
WEEKEND (Sat & Sun) 40/- SEASON (Fri, Sat & Sun) £2.10.0

**Plumpton Racecourse**
Nr. Lewes
MARQUEES
CAMP SITE
CAR PARK
LICENSED BARS
and
REFRESHMENTS

# SUSSEX

Full details and tickets available now from the
**MARQUEE CLUB,**
**90 WARDOUR STREET, W1**
(GER 6601)
also
**Keith Prowse,**
**90 New Bond Street, W1**
(HYD 6000)
Branches and Agents

# AUGUST 8 9 10